THIERRY **BIG T** CORNUET

THE ART OF BBQ

TECHNIQUES & RECIPES, FROM APPETIZERS TO DESSERTS

THIERRY **BIG T** CORNUET

THE ART OF BBQ

TECHNIQUES & RECIPES, FROM APPETIZERS TO DESSERTS

PHOTOGRAPHY BY FABIEN BREUIL

CONTENTS

THE ESSENTIAL ART OF COOKING:
BARBECUING WITH BIG T

In this book, I celebrate the essential art of cooking that I embrace every day. Barbecue possibilities are endless—from appetizers to desserts, from holiday feasts to casual snacks—everything can be made over the flames. This versatility expands our culinary and creative horizons, encouraging us to use the barbecue more often and experiment with a wide range of recipes. The barbecue becomes a true cooking tool in its own right.

In these pages, I champion a culinary philosophy with sharing, authenticity, and generosity at its core. These are the same values I live by every day in my restaurants, and they find their perfect expression in the essential art of cooking on the barbecue.

My own passion for barbecuing started in my backyard, just like yours might have. Now, it's your turn to take charge, dive into these inspiring and flavorful recipes, and unleash the grill master within you.

Let this book guide you on this culinary journey, and help you create unforgettable moments around the barbecue, where great food and good company come together in every bite.

BASIC BARBECUE
PRINCIPLES

Barbecue success hinges on three key factors:

1- HEAT QUALITY

The quality of heat is crucial for even and flawless cooking; this largely depends on the type of charcoal you use (see page 28).

2- FOOD QUALITY

Great barbecue starts where the artisan's work ends! Price isn't the main factor in creating an outstanding meal. Focus on seasonal ingredients, support local farmers, value craftsmanship, and grow your knowledge by talking to the people who supply your food.

3- EXECUTION QUALITY

Your expertise, technique, and creativity are what will make your barbecue extraordinary. To achieve this, you need to understand both direct and indirect cooking methods (see pages 10–11), and master using a meat thermometer to avoid overcooking or undercooking (see page 26).

THE FOUR
COOKING METHODS

DIRECT COOKING

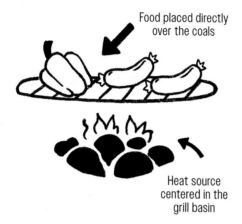

Food placed directly over the coals

Heat source centered in the grill basin

Cooking Type: Intense, quick searing that leaves grill marks. Lid open.

Precautions: Watch out for flames that could burn the food, and try to prevent fat from dripping onto the coals, as this can cause flare-ups.

Specifics: The food is placed on the wire rack directly over the coals and flames.

Result: A crust forms along with caramelization (known as the Maillard reaction), which helps lock in the flavor and juices.

Cooking Temperatures: 355°F–430°F (180°C–220°C).

Recommended For: Finishing or searing all types of food.

INDIRECT COOKING

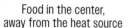

Food in the center, away from the heat source

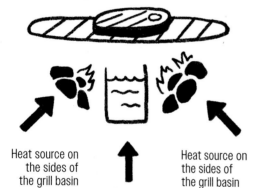

Heat source on the sides of the grill basin

Heat source on the sides of the grill basin

Aluminum pan with a little water

Cooking Type: Slow and even cooking, like a convection oven. Lid closed.

Precautions: Fill the aluminum pan with 2 cups of water and add more if necessary during cooking.

Specifics: The food cooks at a low temperature over a long period.

Result: Tender, melt-in-your-mouth texture.

Cooking Temperatures: 355°F–430°F (180°C–220°C).

Recommended For: Fish, vegetables, sausages, and fatty meat (to prevent fat from dripping onto the coals).

◇ GOOD TO KNOW ◇

What's the purpose of the water pan?

The water helps create moisture inside the barbecue, preventing the food from drying out. It also catches the cooking fat, keeping it from dripping onto the coals. The food should be positioned between two heat sources or on the side opposite the heat.

HOT SMOKING

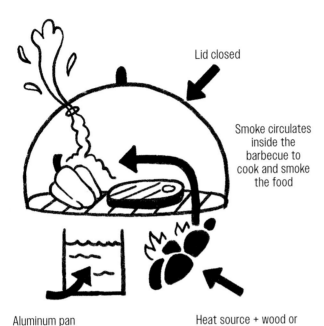

Lid closed

Smoke circulates inside the barbecue to cook and smoke the food

Aluminum pan with a little water

Heat source + wood or wood chips on one side of the grill basin

Cooking Type: This indirect method involves cooking and smoking food simultaneously at a low temperature. Low and slow! Smoking can last anywhere from 45 minutes to several hours.

Precautions: Choose a wood type suited for smoking and the specific foods being smoked.

Specifics: Cooks and smokes at the same time.

Result: Tender, subtly flavored meat.

Cooking Temperatures: 100°F–250°F (40°C–120°C).

Recommended For: Poultry, fish, beef, pork.

◇ GOOD TO KNOW ◇

What's the purpose of the water pan?

As it is for indirect cooking, in cold smoking, the water helps create moisture inside the barbecue, preventing the food from drying out. It also catches the cooking fat, keeping it from dripping onto the coals. The food should be placed between two heat sources or on the side opposite the heat.

COLD SMOKING

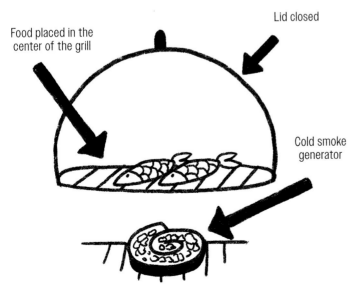

Food placed in the center of the grill

Lid closed

Cold smoke generator

Cooking Type: This indirect method involves only smoking the food, not cooking it. The food remains raw.

Precautions: Choose a wood type suited for smoking and the specific foods being smoked.

Specifics: Smoking is done using aromatic wood chips or sawdust (such as hickory, apple, cherry; see wood types on page 34).

Result: Delicately flavored, subtly colored proteins.

Cooking Temperatures: 60°F–90°F (15°C–30°C).

Recommended For: Fish.

KETTLE **BARBECUE**

Basics

Designed by George Stephen in 1952, the kettle, named for its spherical shape, has earned its place in barbecue history. With its sturdy three-legged base, ergonomic handle, and circular vented lid, it protects your food from wind, flying ashes, and unexpected flare-ups. Lightweight, easy to handle, and accessible, it's a top choice for both beginners and seasoned grill enthusiasts.

SETUP
Set up in a wind-protected area free of flammable materials.

CHOOSING THE FUEL
One of the kettle's major advantages is its versatility: it works equally well with wood, charcoal, or briquettes.

LIGHTING
Use a chimney starter. Place the chimney in the center of the grill, add charcoal, place kindling (like wadded newspaper) underneath, and light it. Once the coals are glowing, pour them into the bottom of the grill basin and remove the chimney.

TEMPERATURE CONTROL
Regulate the airflow and adjust the heat using the vent controls on the grill basin and lid. The lower vents control the air intake, while the upper vents allow heat to escape.

EXTINGUISHING THE KETTLE BARBECUE
After cooking, close the vents to extinguish the fire. About 15 minutes later, the coals will be completely extinguished, allowing you to reuse the remaining charcoal for your next session.

CLEANING AND MAINTENANCE
After each use, put the lid on the kettle to burn off grease and food remnants. Then, scrub the grill grates with a brush to remove any remaining grease, and lightly oil with a neutral oil.

TECHNOLOGY

Connected Kettle

Step into a new era of grilling with Wi-Fi-connected charcoal grills and smokers! Lighting is a breeze, followed by precise temperature adjustment via digital control or a dedicated app. The coals are ready in just 90 seconds, with no effort, fire starters, or additional fuel required.

COOKING METHODS FOR KETTLE BARBECUE

DIRECT COOKING

The food is placed on the wire rack directly over the coals and flames.

Coals in the center of the grill basin

INDIRECT COOKING

Food in the center, away from the coals

Coals on the sides of the grill basin

Aluminum pan with a small amount of water in the center

HOT SMOKING

Lid closed

Food placed opposite the coals

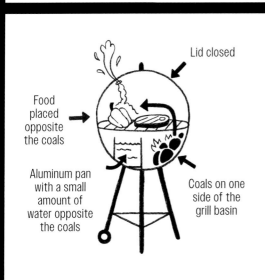

Aluminum pan with a small amount of water opposite the coals

Coals on one side of the grill basin

COLD SMOKING

Food above the smoke generator

Lid closed

Smoke generator in the center of the grill basin

PRACTICAL GUIDE

GAS BARBECUE

Basics

A gas-powered grill (fueled by butane or propane) that heats up quickly without long preheating. It maintains a stable temperature throughout cooking. The gas grill allows for direct cooking, indirect cooking, and both hot and cold smoking.

SETUP

Carefully select an appropriate location. It should be:

· Well-ventilated,

· Free of flammable materials,

· Situated on a flat surface.

Keep safety equipment nearby: fire extinguisher, bucket of water or sand.

Consider the wind direction to avoid smoke nuisance.

LIGHTING THE GAS BARBECUE

1. Open the lid.

2. Carefully connect the fuel (butane or propane) tank.

3. Open the tank valve(s).

4. Prime the regulator by pressing the primer button, if needed.

5. Turn the main burner knob slightly and allow gas to flow for a few seconds.

6. Light the barbecue by pressing the igniter to spark the ignition.

7. Let the barbecue heat up with the lid closed for 10 to 15 minutes before starting to cook.

EXTINGUISHING THE GAS BARBECUE

1. Turn off the burners.

2. Close the fuel tank valve(s).

3. Disconnect the regulator by unscrewing or unclipping it.

Store the butane or propane tanks outside or in a well-ventilated area.

CLEANING AND MAINTENANCE

After each use, thoroughly clean the barbecue to prevent wear and corrosion. Cover it with a protective cover if left outside.

SAFETY

⚠ Do not move the appliance while it's on or if food is cooking on it. To ensure safe operation, avoid lighting the barbecue in windy conditions.

GOOD TO KNOW

Which Fuel to Choose: Butane or Propane?

For optimal performance, opt for propane if possible; it is known for its heating power and resistance to low temperatures.

Whichever you choose, be sure it is hooked up and turned on and off properly.

COOKING METHODS FOR GAS BARBECUE

TECHNICAL DETAILS

DIRECT COOKING

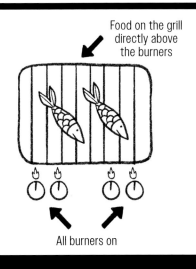

Food on the grill directly above the burners

All burners on

INDIRECT COOKING

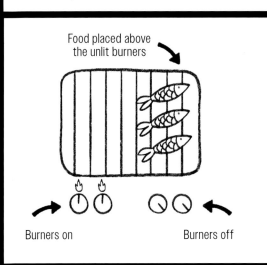

Food placed above the unlit burners

Burners on   Burners off

HOT SMOKING

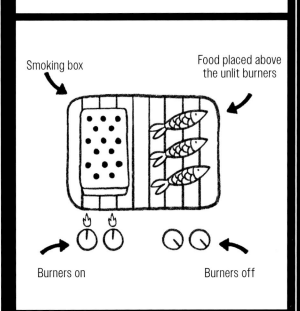

Smoking box

Food placed above the unlit burners

Burners on   Burners off

COLD SMOKING

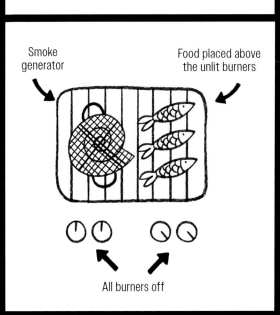

Smoke generator

Food placed above the unlit burners

All burners off

PRACTICAL GUIDE

PELLET BARBECUE

Basics

The pellet barbecue operates by burning wood pellets, which are automatically fed into the grill via an auger. The pellets impart a delightful smoky flavor to the food. Once the lid is closed, a fan ensures even circulation of smoke and heat, resulting in consistent cooking. The food remains moist, tender, and flavorful. This barbecue is primarily designed for indirect cooking and hot smoking.

SETUP

Carefully select an appropriate location. It should be:
- Clear of any flammable materials,
- Situated on a flat surface (patio or garden),
- Sheltered from drafts.

Keep safety equipment within reach: fire extinguisher, bucket of water or sand.

FILLING THE HOPPER

The hopper is the pellet storage container for the barbecue. Fill the hopper with food-grade wood pellets according to the manufacturer's instructions. Be careful not to overfill the hopper to avoid overflow.

LIGHTING THE PELLET BARBECUE

Connect the barbecue to a power source and turn it on according to the manufacturer's instructions. Typically, just pressing a start button begins the process.

TEMPERATURE ADJUSTMENT

Use the control screen to set the desired cooking temperature. Ensure you select the appropriate temperature for the recipe and ingredients.

COOKING

Once the barbecue has reached the desired temperature, you can start cooking:
- Place the food on the grill or in the combustion chamber (depending on the barbecue model),
- Regularly monitor the food during cooking. Adjust the temperature if necessary, using the control screen and the provided probe.

CLEANING AND MAINTENANCE

To keep the pellet barbecue running well, do the following after each use:
- Turn off the barbecue,
- Let it cool completely before cleaning,
- Empty the hopper of any remaining pellets,
- Remove the ashes from the combustion chamber,
- Clean the cooking grill,
- Empty the grease tray.

TIP FROM BIG T

Which Pellets to Choose?

- Apple: poultry, pork, vegetables, cheeses
- Cherry: poultry, pork, beef, cheeses
- Hickory: beef, poultry, pork, vegetables
- Mesquite: beef, poultry, fish
- Maple: pork, beef, poultry, vegetables, fish
- Acacia: cheeses, vegetables, meat, poultry, fish

COOKING METHODS FOR PELLET BARBECUE

INDIRECT COOKING AND HOT SMOKING

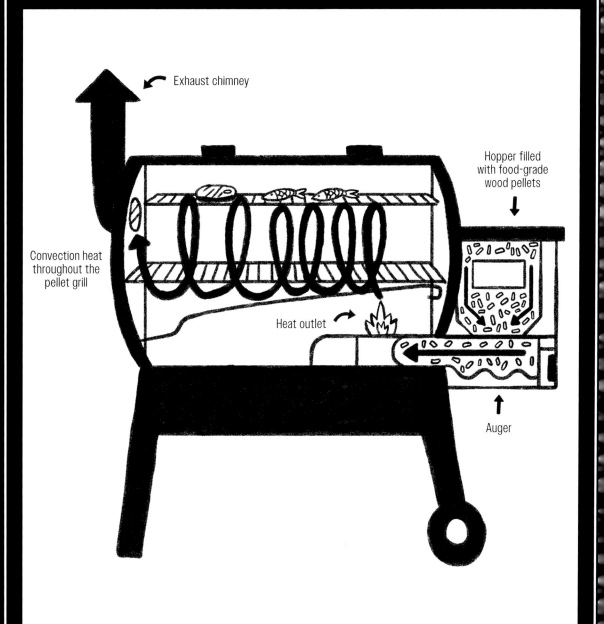

Exhaust chimney

Hopper filled with food-grade wood pellets

Convection heat throughout the pellet grill

Heat outlet

Auger

KAMADO **BARBECUE**

Basics

The kamado is an egg-shaped barbecue of Japanese origin, reportedly brought to the United States by Americans after World War II. It allows for direct and indirect cooking, as well as smoking. Due to its ovoid shape, hot air circulates uniformly within the barbecue, mimicking the function of a convection oven.

WHAT FUEL TO USE?

Fire Starters

Use natural fire starters or opt for simple, effective, and safe solutions such as:

· Wool or cotton balls coated with wax or vegetable fat,

· Compressed wood cubes,

· Electric fire starters (ideally a "torch" type, which blows a stream of superheated air to create a combustion point, for guaranteed quick-glowing coals!).

Avoid

· Chemical products (such as lighter fluid or charcoal briquettes with additives). They alter the taste of the food and are harmful to health.

· Alcohol, flammable liquids, or gels. The ceramic is porous and can absorb them, giving the food an unpleasant taste.

· Paper and cardboard. They produce volatile ashes that can land on your food during cooking.

CAN I USE A CHIMNEY STARTER?
No! A chimney starter could create thermal shock and damage the ceramic, a material sensitive to abrupt temperature changes. The ceramic must gradually heat up alongside the fire. Additionally, the charcoal basket and natural air draft of a kamado already offer quick, simple, and safe ignition.

WHAT CHARCOAL TO CHOOSE?

You should choose it based on the cooking method (direct or indirect).

For Direct Cooking

Opt for restaurant-grade quality charcoal because:

· Its excellent calorific value ensures quick ignition and lasts about 1 hour;

· Large pieces promote air circulation and thus better combustion.

For Indirect Cooking or Hot Smoking

Opt for Argentine charcoal because:

· The size and density of the pieces affect the amount of heat produced and the fire's longevity;

· Once the coals are lit, they can last 4–5 hours (and even up to 17 hours around 194°F or 90°C).

Avoid

· Briquettes. The dust produced by their combustion can clog the pores of the ceramic, giving dishes an unpleasant flavor.

· Wood. This fuel produces too intense a heat, which risks damaging the barbecue. The ceramic may crack or even break!

EXTINGUISHING THE KAMADO

To extinguish a kamado, it must be deprived of oxygen. Close the lid and both ventilation flaps. Do not open the barbecue for about 20 minutes; otherwise, the fire might reignite! Never extinguish the kamado with water! This would cause thermal shock that could break the ceramic.

TECHNICAL DETAILS

COOKING METHODS FOR KAMADO BARBECUE

DIRECT COOKING

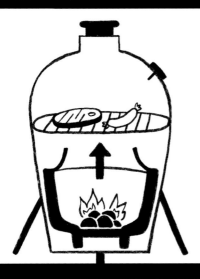

INDIRECT COOKING/ HOT SMOKING

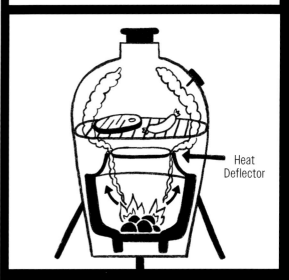

Heat Deflector

ADJUSTING THE INTERNAL TEMPERATURE

Adjusting the kamado barbecue's temperature happens by controlling air coming in and out—through the top and bottom vents. The more open the vents are, the more heat is created, and conversely, mostly closed vents will result in less heat. Once the vents are open (or opened slightly), the grill will continue to heat for a few minutes before the temperature stabilizes. If you find your grill is too hot, you can simply close the vents more to reduce airflow; again, it will take a few minutes for the temperature to stabilize.

CLEANING AND MAINTENANCE

After grilling, close the lid and the vents; the barbecue will warm up again and burn off any food residue, then it will start to cool down. It can take several hours for the grill to cool completely. Scrub the grill with a brush to remove excess grease, and oil the grill well with a neutral oil.

TIP FROM BIG T

When opening the grill lid to check on food, do it in two stages: lift slightly and hold for 3–4 seconds. Then open it all the way. Opening the lid fully all at once can cause a surge of oxygen and a big flare-up.

BRASERO
PLANCHA/BRAZIER

Basics

The brasero plancha (brazier) is a cooking plate made of steel or cast iron, fueled by a wood fire or charcoal. Opt for braseros between 28 and 36 inches (70 to 92 cm) in diameter, with a fire pit of about 14 inches (35 cm) in diameter. Beyond 40 inches (100 cm) in diameter, you'll need a large amount of wood consumption to effectively heat the plate. The plate should be at least ½ inch (10 mm) thick. The thicker it is, the more heat it will require, but thickness also provides more even heating. The brasero plancha allows you to cook different foods on various heat zones. By using a grill positioned in the center above the fire, you can grill food at the beginning or end of cooking. You can also hang food for slow cooking.

SETUP

Carefully select an appropriate location. It should be:
· Clear of any flammable materials,
· Situated on a flat surface (patio or garden).

Keep safety equipment within reach: fire extinguisher, bucket of water or sand.

Consider the wind direction to avoid smoke nuisance.

CHOOSING THE FUEL

For quality coals, opt for logs of hardwood (oak, beech, or birch). For lighting, birch sap fire starters and dry twigs are best.

Avoid
· Resinous woods (pine, fir, juniper, etc.),
· Flammable products (methylated spirits or ethanol).

LIGHTING AND HEATING UP

Place the fire starter or twigs under the dry logs. Light the fire starter or twigs from below using a match or lighter. Allow 30 to 60 minutes for the steel cooking plate to reach optimal temperature, usually between 390°F and 575°F (200°C and 300°C). Some models are equipped with air flow management systems to speed up this process.

PREPARING THE COOKING PLATE

Before the first use, apply a thin layer of vegetable oil to the cooking plate and gradually bring it up to temperature. This step helps "season" the plate, preventing grease from running off the edges. You can create cooking zones by distributing the coals according to your needs.

HOW TO MAINTAIN THE RIGHT TEMPERATURE

Load the fire pit to the maximum and regularly add wood. The plate should be between 300°F and 395°F (150°C and 200°C).

EXTINGUISHING THE BRAZIER (BRASERO PLANCHA)

Let the fire gradually die out. At the very end, wet the coals to ensure they are completely extinguished.

CLEANING AND MAINTENANCE

After use, clean the hot cooking plate with a stainless steel or wooden spatula to remove food residue. If necessary, use ice cubes to loosen stubborn residues. Finally, oil the cooking plate with a cloth to protect it from corrosion and prepare it for the next use.

COOKING METHODS FOR BRAZIER (BRASERO PLANCHA)

DIRECT COOKING, INDIRECT COOKING, AND HOT SMOKING

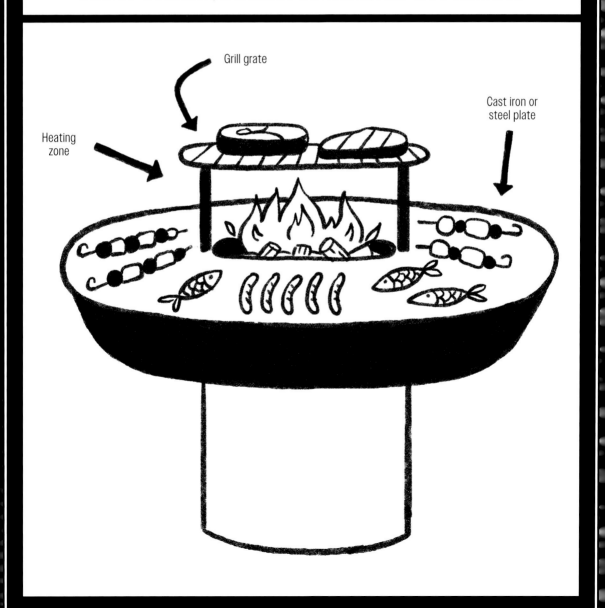

Grill grate

Cast iron or steel plate

Heating zone

PRACTICAL GUIDE

THE TEMPERATURE
OF FOOD

**The key to perfect cooking lies in one essential factor:
the internal temperature of the food.**

THE ESSENTIAL TOOL

For any serious griller, investing in a probe thermometer (meat thermometer) is crucial! Some are very affordable (starting at around $45). If you prefer a bit more precision and technology, you can opt for a Bluetooth thermometer (around $100), which allows you to monitor the internal temperature in real time.

HOW TO USE THE THERMOMETER

Insert the thermometer into the thickest part of the food without touching the bone (if it's meat) or the spine (if it's a whole fish). If it's fruit, the pit doesn't matter. Repeat as necessary, or leave the thermometer in the food if it's designed to stay in during cooking.

COOKING TEMPERATURES

The chart opposite lists the ideal internal temperatures for each food group, regardless of the cut.

COOKING TEMPERATURES
BY BIG T

COOKING
TABLE

MEATS

	RARE	MEDIUM-RARE	MEDIUM	GROUND
LAMB	125°F (52°C)	135°F (57°C)	150°F (66°C)	—
BEEF	125°F (52°C)	135°F (57°C)	150°F (66°C)	160°F (71°C)
PORK	—	145°F (63°C)	150°F (66°C)	160°F (71°C)
VEAL	125°F (52°C)	135°F (57°C)	150°F (66°C)	160°F (71°C)

POULTRY

	BREAST	THIGH/LEG	LEG	GROUND
CHICKEN	165°F (74°C) (white meat)	170°F (77°C)	—	175°F (79°C)
DUCK	140°F (60°C) (magret)	—	165°F (74°C)	—

FISH AND SHELLFISH

Cod (fillet)	130°F (54°C)
Whole Sea Bream	140°F (60°C)
Halibut (fillet)	125°F (52°C)
Lobster (tail)	120–130°F (49–54°C)
Spiny Lobster (tail)	120–130°F (49–54°C)
Sea Bass	140°F (60°C)
Scallops	125°F (52°C)
Arctic Char	140°F (60°C)
Perch/Zander (fillet)	135°F (57°C)
Salmon	120–130°F (49–54°C)
Tuna	120–125°F (49–52°C) or raw in the center
Turbot (fillet)	120-125°F (49-52°C)

Fish and shellfish have delicate, moist flesh.

Their cooking is quick and must be precise, with perfectly controlled heat.

FRUITS AND VEGETABLES

VEGETABLES
Al dente texture: 180°F (83°C)
Tender texture: above 185°F (85°C)

FRUITS
Al dente texture: 180°F (83°C)
Tender texture: above 185°F (85°C),
except for pineapple and plums:
170°F (75°C) for a tender texture.

PRACTICAL

GUIDE

CHARCOAL

Selecting the right charcoal is crucial for a successful barbecue. Although eco-friendly alternatives offer innovative solutions, traditional charcoal is often preferable for its cost-effectiveness and proven reliability. However, the emergence of these alternatives signifies a positive shift towards more environmentally friendly practices in outdoor cooking.

HOW TO CHOOSE THE RIGHT CHARCOAL?

The best method is to read the information on the bag. Quality (restaurant-grade) charcoal should have:

· Large pieces or chunks that are clean (free from dust and additives),

· A fixed carbon content of more than 82%,

· A moisture content of less than 5%,

· A lighting time of no more than 20 minutes,

· A burn time of at least 50 minutes.

WHICH CHARCOAL FOR WHICH USE?

Match the type of charcoal to your needs:

· Quick Grilling (sausages or skewers): Soft charcoal that heats up quickly and intensely.

· Larger Cuts of Meat (whole chicken or ribeye): Hard charcoal that provides extended combustion for perfect cooking.

· Argentine Charcoal: Allows for slow and even cooking.

· Bamboo Charcoal: Regulates external moisture (e.g., if it rains).

· Coconut Charcoal: Guarantees prolonged burning.

TIP FROM BIG T

My favorite charcoal comes from Grill O'Bois, a French company in operation since 1975, which puts care for the environment at the forefront of their practices.

Alternatives to Charcoal

In recent years, a range of eco-friendly and environmentally conscious charcoal alternatives has emerged, allowing for more sustainable grilling. Despite their appeal, these options often come at a higher price or offer variable performance, so traditional charcoal remains popular. Here's an overview of the most reputable alternative options:

Briquettes

They are a good choice for closed barbecues.

It's important to note that they heat up less quickly and less intensely than traditional charcoal chunks due to their compactness.

To achieve a good fire, use the same amount of briquettes as you would charcoal chunks, approximately 1 gallon (about 4 liters) of briquettes for about 2.5 pounds (1 kg of wood).

· Coconut Shell Briquettes: Up to 3 hours of cooking without wood, fully natural, ideal for grilling.

· Olive Pit Briquettes: Made from olive residues, they light up quickly, burn for a long time, and emit little smoke. They preserve natural resources and are odorless and tasteless.

Grapevine Cuttings

They can be used as the main fuel or alongside charcoal, adding a delightful smoky flavor to grilled foods.

Corn Cobs

They light easily, do not affect the taste of grilled food, and help preserve forests. However, their calorific value is relatively limited, making them more suited for kindling or quick cooking.

THE ART OF
SMOKING

Basics

An ancient method once used for preserving food, smoking is now widely recognized for its remarkable flavor attributes. Smoking involves slowly cooking food between 60°F–215°F (15°C–100°C) while exposing it to smoke from a wood fire. This exposure imparts a distinct flavor that is unmatched by any other cooking method. Hot smoking allows for slow cooking of food between 100°F–250°F (40°C–120°C). Cold smoking, with temperatures below 85°F (30°C), is ideal for preserving food. Here are some tips for achieving artisanal smoking, even without a specialized smoker.

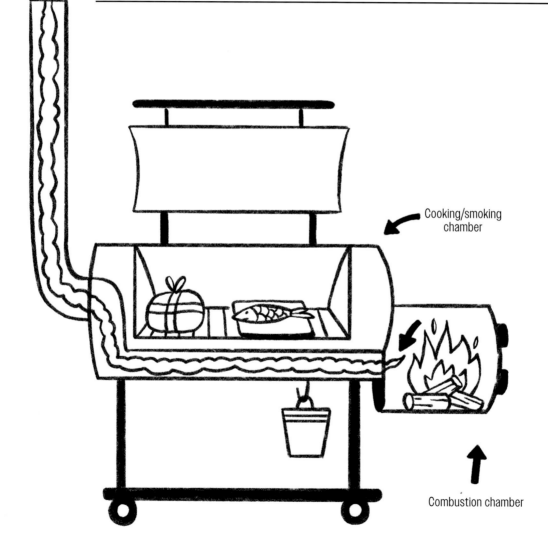

Cooking/smoking chamber

Combustion chamber

WHICH BARBECUE FOR SMOKING?

Gas Barbecue

Buying a smoker is not mandatory. For beginners, a propane barbecue equipped with a smoking box (see p. 32) can be perfectly suitable. This approach offers the advantage of testing the method at a lower cost. Place the smoking box on the heat zone at maximum heat until smoke emerges. Reduce the heat as low as possible to maintain a constant smoke. Place the meat in the center of the barbecue, above the closed burners.

Charcoal Barbecue

All types of charcoal barbecues are suitable for smoking. Place the charcoal on one side of the barbecue, and the meat above an area without charcoal. Then add 1 to 3 pieces of wood directly to the charcoal, depending on the amount of meat on the barbecue. You can presoak the wood to add extra moisture and achieve a denser smoke.

Smoker

A smoker offers precise control of temperature and smoke, whether hot or cold.

Pellet Barbecue

Valued for its versatility, the pellet barbecue allows for slow cooking and can be used for both hot and cold smoking. Additionally, it offers a wide range of flavors depending on the types of pellets used.

> ### TIP FROM BIG T
> ## An Essential
> Using a meat thermometer is recommended when smoking to monitor the temperature of the food.

> ### TIP FROM BIG T
> ## A Pitfall to Avoid
> The most common mistake people make when smoking is using excessive smoke—starting with a moderate amount is best. With a charcoal barbecue, aim for almost transparent smoke using wood chunks rather than chips. With a gas barbecue, controlling smoke density is trickier due to limited air circulation. Check the smoke color before placing the food on the grill. It should be white. Black smoke will impart a bitter taste to food.

WHAT TO SMOKE?

For beginners, it is advisable to start with simple meat, such as chicken drumsticks or pork tenderloin. Chicken requires less smoke than pork, but make sure to use a meat thermometer in both cases. Then, develop your expertise with fish and cheeses.

SMOKING TIME

It varies depending on the type of food.

- For each 1.75 ounces (50 g) of pork or beef, allow 1–1 ½ hours of smoking.

- For larger cuts, it is best to turn them every 2–3 hours and salt them regularly. As you approach the end of cooking, monitor the meat to avoid overcooking.

MAKING A
SMOKING BOX

In the absence of a dedicated smoker,
you can create a rudimentary smoking box.

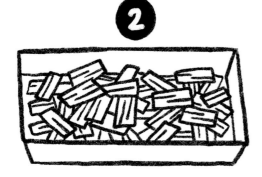

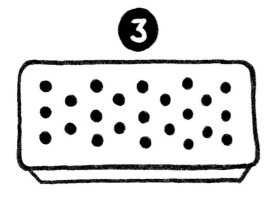

MATERIALS

· 1 aluminum container, 4 x 8 inches (10 x 20 cm)
· 9–10 ½ ounces (250–300 g) aromatic wood chips (for hot smoking) or smoking sawdust (for cold smoking)
· Aluminum foil

PREPARING THE BOX

1. Soak the wood chips in 1 quart (1 l) cold water for 1 hour to moisten them.

2. Fill the aluminum container with the moistened wood chips.

3. Cover the container with aluminum foil, and poke about 15 holes in the foil (to allow airflow for proper combustion).

SMOKING

4. Place the smoking box on the heat zone at maximum heat until smoke begins to emerge (about 20 to 30 minutes). Place the food on the opposite side and close the lid.

5. Check the temperature of the smoker. It should be between 175°F–275°F (80°C–135°C), depending on the food and its thickness.

6. Let the food smoke for the time indicated in the recipe, ensuring a constant supply of fuel. Open the smoker (to check food) a maximum of two times during cooking.

PRACTICAL GUIDE

WOOD FOR SMOKING

Here are some commonly used types of wood for smoking meat, fish, cheeses, and vegetables, each imparting a unique flavor:

BEECH: Classic elegance. A traditional choice for a subtle and refined flavor. Mild smoke, perfect for fish and cheeses.

OAK: Robustness assured. Impresses without overpowering, offering a deep flavor. Rich smoke, ideal for meats like beef or lamb.

ORANGE AND LEMON: Exotic freshness. Provides a refreshing and distinctive taste experience. Smoke with light citrus notes, ideal for delicate fish.

OLIVE: Mediterranean in smoke. Sunny and distinctive aroma that enhances dishes. Savory touch, perfect for poultry and vegetables.

MAPLE: Fine and sweet lightness. Delicate aromas for a smooth taste experience. Subtle flavor, ideal for fish, poultry, and hams.

HICKORY: Stunning intensity. Brings a distinctive, powerful taste. Strong aromas, perfect for red meats and game.

CHERRY: Fruity sweetness. Exquisite flavors with a slight sweet note and amazing color. Ideal for pork, lamb, white meats, seafood, vegetables, and cheeses.

MESQUITE: Robust aroma, distinctive flavor. Elevates each bite to new heights of taste pleasure. Unmatched for enhancing meat, particularly beef.

APPLE: Sophisticated versatility. Subtle fruity accents. A taste experience marked by elegance and refinement. Perfect harmony with a variety of meats (beef, poultry, pork, lamb) and cheeses.

WOOD TYPES
BY FOOD GROUPS

TABLE OF
WOOD TYPES

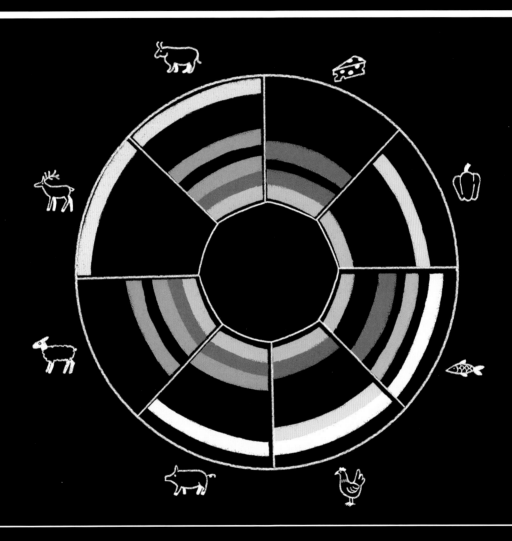

Cherry: Pork, lamb, veal, poultry, seafood, vegetables, cheeses

Apple: Beef, poultry, pork, lamb, cheeses

Mesquite: Beef, lamb, pork, veal

Beech: Fish, cheeses

Oak: Beef, lamb

Orange and Lemon: Fish

Olive: Poultry, vegetables

Maple: Fish, poultry, ham

Hickory: Beef, game

ACCESSORIES

CHARCOAL STARTER - 1
It facilitates the starting of the barbecue. This safe and efficient solution allows for perfect coals in less than 20 minutes.

BARBECUE GRIDDLE - 2
With its smooth surface, this option allows for cooking small items without the risk of losing them between the grates, while retaining marinades for an explosion of flavors.

SMOKER BOX FOR GAS BBQ - 3
Filled with smoking wood chips, this box imparts subtle and authentic flavors that add a unique aroma to the grilled food.

COLD SMOKE GENERATOR - 4
Filled with aromatic wood shavings, it disperses subtle and authentic flavors that add a unique aroma to the smoke.

COOKING THERMOMETER - 5
Whether simple or connected, this accessory allows for controlling the internal temperature of the food, ensuring perfect cooking.

CUTTING BOARD - 6
Made from quality hardwood (beech, birch, bamboo, or walnut), it provides a stable and sturdy surface for precise cutting and preserves the sharpness of knives.

COOKING UTENSILS - 7
Tongs, spatulas, and forks are essential for turning, moving, and serving food with ease and efficiency.

KNIVES - 8
Three knives are essential for the barbecue: the brisket knife, for slicing thin slices of cooked meat or smoked fish; the Serbian knife, for cutting meat, vegetables, and fish, with the blade side used as a tenderizer; and the chef's knife, capable of slicing, chopping, dicing, and trimming with remarkable precision.

Cast Iron Cookware

They offer great versatility for barbecuing, rivaling the performance of a kitchen oven. They can be placed directly on the barbecue grate or on the fire pit plate, whether for indirect or direct cooking. Cast iron is known for its durability and ability to distribute heat evenly, ensuring optimal cooking results even under extreme heat conditions. It is easy to clean, facilitating maintenance of the cookware after each use.

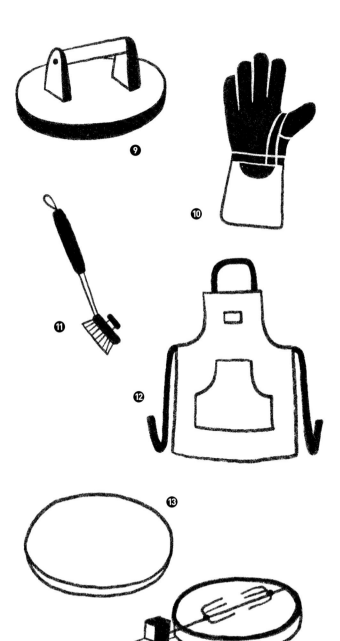

MEAT PRESS - 9
It ensures even cooking for perfect snacks: from juicy burgers to crispy paninis, this versatile tool guarantees chef-worthy results.

HEAT-RESISTANT GLOVES - 10
They are essential for ensuring safety during a barbecue session as they provide optimal protection against intense heat, reducing the risk of burns. They come in leather and synthetic fabric.

CLEANING BRUSH - 11
It helps remove grease and food debris, ensuring the cleanliness and durability of the barbecue.

COVER
It protects the barbecue from the elements and dust, extending its lifespan.

BUTCHER PAPER
Used for long cooking times on the barbecue or in the oven. It helps retain meat juices and creates a crispy crust during cooking. In contrast, in aluminum foil, the meat's outer crust softens.

LEATHER APRON - 12
It provides protection against heat and splashes. Choose an apron with double-stitched seams and rivets for greater durability.

PIZZA STONE - 13
This solution allows for quick and crispy cooking of homemade pizzas, replicating the result of a traditional pizza oven.

ROTISSERIE AND SPIT - 14
These versatile accessories allow for making a variety of recipes, perfectly grilled, from juicy roast chicken to tasty kebabs.

SMALL BITES

SMOKED TUNA RILLETTES
WITH MULTIGRAIN TOAST

Preparation: 25 minutes
Cooking Time: 30 minutes
Cooking Type: Indirect heat

Equipment
Smoking box, smoking wood chips
 (apple or maple)

Type of BBQ
Gas, pellet, charcoal, kamado,
 smoker

Makes
4 servings

Ingredients
2 (5- to 6-ounce/140- to 150-g)
 cans tuna in oil
Zest and juice of 2 lemons
9 ounces (250 g) cream cheese,
 at room temperature
1 bunch chives, finely chopped
1 bunch cilantro, finely chopped
1 bunch parsley, finely chopped
2 red onions, finely chopped
2 shallots, finely chopped
1 loaf multigrain bread, sliced

Set up your BBQ for smoking by adding wood chips to your smoking box. Open the tuna cans, leaving the lids slightly attached, and place them in the smoker or near the smoking box. Close the BBQ lid and smoke the tuna for 30 minutes.

Transfer the tuna to a large mixing bowl. If you would like to use the empty cans as serving cups, return the empty cans to the grill or smoker for another 15–20 minutes. Allow them to cool to room temperature.

To the mixing bowl with the tuna, add the lemon zest and juice to taste. Flake the tuna with a fork, then stir in the cream cheese until smooth. Add chives, cilantro, parsley, red onions, and shallots. Mix well.

Toast the sliced bread on the grill until golden. Serve the smoked tuna rillettes spread over the toasted bread.

SARDINES WITH CARAMELIZED PEPPERS
ON LEMON-BUTTER TOAST

Preparation Time: 20 minutes
Cooking Time: 1 hour
Cooking Type: Direct +
indirect heat

Equipment
Cast iron skillet

Type of BBQ
Gas, pellet, charcoal, brazier,
    smoker

Makes
4 servings

Ingredients:
2 red onions
2 mini red bell peppers
2 mini yellow bell peppers
4 garlic cloves, peeled
Olive oil
Kosher salt and freshly ground
    black pepper
Maple syrup
1 tablespoon unsalted butter,
    at room temperature
Zest of 1 lemon
2 thick slices country bread
8 fresh sardines (5–7 ounces
    or 150–200 g each)
Smoked sea salt

Peel the onions and slice them into rings. Place them in the cast iron skillet along with the bell peppers and garlic cloves. Drizzle with olive oil and season to taste with salt and pepper and a splash of maple syrup. Cook on the grill over indirect heat for about an hour, stirring occasionally, until everything is caramelized and flavorful.

In a small bowl, mix the butter and lemon zest. Toast the bread slices on the grill until golden brown on both sides. Spread the lemon butter on one side of the hot bread and set aside.

Coat the sardines lightly in olive oil and grill for 1 minute per side, just until seared.

Top the toasted bread with the caramelized onion mixture and grilled sardines. Drizzle with olive oil and sprinkle with smoked sea salt. Cut each piece of bread in two to make 4 servings.

Tip from BIG T

To add some kick to the toasts, drizzle with chile oil instead of olive oil.

SMOKED BEET
DIP

Preparation Time: 15 minutes
Cooking Time: 45 minutes
Cooking Type: Direct heat

Equipment
Blender, BBQ tongs

Type of BBQ
Gas, pellet, charcoal, kamado,
  smoker

Makes
4 servings

Ingredients:
2 medium unpeeled beets
Olive oil
A few sprigs thyme
A few sprigs each chives, parsley,
  and cilantro
5 ounces (150 g) cream cheese,
  at room temperature
Juice of 1 lemon
Smoked sea salt and freshly ground
  black pepper
Corn or flour tortillas or chips,
  for dipping

Prepare a bed of coals in your BBQ. Place the unpeeled beets on a large sheet of aluminum foil and drizzle with olive oil. Add the thyme sprigs and wrap the foil to enclose the beets. Place the foil-wrapped beets directly on the coals and cook for 45 minutes, turning every 15 minutes, until tender.

While the beets are cooking, finely chop the chives, parsley, and cilantro.

In a mixing bowl, combine the cream cheese and lemon juice until smooth. Stir in the chopped herbs.

Once the beets are tender, remove them from the coals, unwrap them, and let them cool. Peel the beets and blend until smooth, then add to the cream cheese mixture and stir to combine. Season with smoked salt and pepper to taste.

Serve with tortillas or chips.

Tip from BIG T

For a fun twist, make your own chips by cutting tortillas into triangles and grilling them.

HUMMUS
BY PALMYRA

Preparation Time: 15 minutes
Cooking Time: 1 hour 30 minutes
Cooking Type: Indirect heat

Equipment	Type of BBQ	Makes
Cast iron pot, food processor, smoking box	Gas, pellet, charcoal, kamado, smoker	6 servings

Ingredients

1 ½ cups (300 g) cooked chickpeas
3 tablespoons olive oil, plus more for serving
Juice of 1 lime
2 tablespoons tahini
1 red chile pepper, finely chopped
1 tablespoon ground cumin
1 tablespoon ground coriander
1 garlic clove, peeled
1 teaspoon kosher salt
Freshly ground black pepper
Paprika, for serving
Pita bread, for serving

Preheat your BBQ in smoker mode. In a cast iron pot, mix the chickpeas and the olive oil. Place the cast iron pot on the grill over indirect heat and smoke the chickpeas for 1 hour and 30 minutes at 110°F (45°C).

Transfer the smoked chickpeas to the bowl of the food processor and blend until smooth. Add the lime juice, tahini, chile pepper, cumin, coriander, and garlic. Blend until well combined. Season with the salt and add pepper to taste.

Serve the hummus in a bowl, garnished with a sprinkle of paprika and a drizzle of olive oil. Serve with warm pita bread.

TZATZIKI
WITH PICKLED CUCUMBERS

Preparation Time: 15 minutes
Marinating Time: 2 days
Cooking Time: 1 hour 30 minutes
Cooking Type: Indirect heat

Equipment	Type of BBQ	Makes
Cast iron pot, smoking box	Gas, pellet, charcoal, kamado, smoker	6 servings

Ingredients
Pickled Cucumbers

½ cup (125 ml) apple cider vinegar
⅓ cup (75 g) brown sugar
2 English cucumbers
4 coriander seeds

Tzatziki

4 tablespoons olive oil, divided
2 garlic cloves, unpeeled
1 cup (250 g) Greek yogurt
1 bunch mint, chopped
Juice of 1 lime
½ teaspoon kosher salt
Pita bread, for serving

Pickled cucumbers (prepare 2 days ahead): In a saucepan, combine the apple cider vinegar, brown sugar, and 1 cup water, and bring to a boil, stirring to dissolve the sugar. Turn off the heat. Thinly slice the cucumbers and place them in a jar. Add the coriander seeds. Pour the hot liquid over the cucumbers, let cool, then refrigerate for 2 days.

On the day of serving: Preheat the BBQ. Drain the pickled cucumbers and place them in a cast iron pot. Add 2 tablespoons of the olive oil and the unpeeled garlic cloves. Smoke over indirect heat for 1 hour and 30 minutes at 110°F (45°C).

Peel the smoked garlic cloves and place in a mixing bowl. Mash them with a fork, then add the yogurt, the remaining 2 tablespoons olive oil, mint, lime juice, and salt.

Cut the smoked cucumbers into small pieces and stir into the yogurt mixture. Serve chilled with pita bread.

SWEET & SPICY
SAUSAGE
BITES

Preparation Time: 15 minutes
Marinade Time: 24 hours
Cooking Time: 25 minutes
Cooking Type: Indirect heat

Equipment
Food processor, injection syringe
  (optional)

Type of BBQ
Gas, pellet, charcoal, kamado,
  smoker, brazier

Makes
6 servings

Ingredients:
2 red chile peppers, stemmed
½ cup (120 ml) bourbon
15 mini chorizo sausage links
1 tablespoon BBQ Dry Rub
  (see page 257) or Texas rub
3 tablespoons maple syrup
"Got You Babe" BBQ Sauce
  (see page 252), for serving

In the food processor, blend the chile peppers with the bourbon.

If using an injection syringe, divide the bourbon-chile mixture and inject half into the chorizos, then pour the remaining mixture into a resealable bag (if you don't have an injection syringe, put all the bourbon-chile mixture in the bag). Add the dry rub mix and maple syrup. Add the chorizos, seal the bag, and marinate in the refrigerator for 24 hours.

Preheat the BBQ. Grill the chorizos on indirect heat for 25 minutes.

Brush with BBQ sauce before serving.

Tip from BIG T

Using an injection syringe flavors the meat from the inside, giving it an exceptional taste.

FREESTYLE BEEF
NACHOS

Preparation Time: 20 minutes
Rest Time: 15 minutes
Cooking Time: 15 minutes
Cooking Type: Direct + indirect heat

Equipment
Cast iron skillet, grill plate or griddle

Type of BBQ
Gas, pellet, charcoal, kamado, smoker, brazier

Makes
4 servings

Ingredients:
9 ounces (250 g) ground beef
4 tablespoons BBQ Dry Rub
  (see page 257)
4 yellow onions, diced
4 bell peppers, diced
½ cup (50 g) canned corn
Olive oil
2 tablespoons bourbon
1 small red chile pepper, stemmed,
  seeded, and thinly sliced
9 ounces (250 g) tortilla chips
⅔ cup (150 g) sour cream
1½ cups (150 g) grated cheddar
  cheese
1½ cups (150 g) grated mozzarella
  cheese

Season the ground beef with the dry rub and let it rest for 15 minutes while you preheat the BBQ.

Place the cast iron skillet on the grill over direct heat. When it is hot, add the onions and bell peppers and dry until slightly charred. Add the corn and cook for 5 more minutes. Remove from the skillet and set aside.

In the same skillet, add a drizzle of olive oil and the ground beef. Cook, stirring, until browned. Add the bourbon, then stir in the sautéed vegetables and the chile pepper.

On the grill plate or griddle, layer the tortilla chips, the beef mixture, sour cream, and grated cheese. Repeat layers if necessary, ending with cheese on top. Place on the grill over indirect heat and cook for 15 minutes, until cheese is melted and ingredients are warmed through.

BBQ CHICKEN
DRUMSTICKS

Preparation Time: 30 minutes
Cooking Time: 1 hour 15 minutes
Cooking Type: Indirect heat

Equipment
Cast iron skillet, meat thermometer

Type of BBQ
Gas, pellet, charcoal, kamado, smoker

Makes
4–6 servings

Ingredients:
8–12 chicken drumsticks
5 tablespoons Chicken Dry Rub
  (see page 256)
1 tablespoon vegetable oil
½ yellow onion, finely chopped
2 garlic cloves, minced
3 teaspoons smoked paprika
Chili powder
½ cup (120 g) tomato paste
¼ cup (60 ml) maple syrup
1 tablespoon apple cider vinegar
1 tablespoon balsamic vinegar
1 tablespoon soy sauce
"Got You Babe" BBQ Sauce
  (see page 252), for serving

Preheat the BBQ. Trim the ends of the drumsticks to release the skin, gently loosen the skin from the meat without removing the skin, then wrap the ends in foil. Season the exposed meat with dry rub, then reposition the skin.

Stand the drumsticks upright (bone facing up) on the grill (see Tip) over indirect heat. Cook for 40 minutes to 1 hour, until the meat reaches an internal temperature of 170°F (76°C).

While the chicken is cooking, make the sauce: in the cast iron skillet over indirect heat, warm the oil and sauté the onion and garlic for 2 minutes, until aromatic. Add the smoked paprika and a pinch of chili powder and cook for 5–6 minutes. Stir in the tomato paste and 1 cup (225 ml) water, then add the maple syrup, apple cider vinegar, balsamic vinegar, and soy sauce. Simmer for 15 minutes, stirring occasionally.

Dip the drumsticks in the BBQ sauce and return to the grill for 15 minutes to caramelize. Serve with extra sauce or "Got You Babe" sauce.

Tip from BIG T

Use a drumstick rack to keep the chicken upright during cooking.

SMOKED TROUT STUFFED
WITH CREAM CHEESE

Preparation Time: 15 minutes
Soaking Time: 4 hours
Cooking Time: 15 minutes
Cooking Type: Indirect heat

Equipment
Cedar plank, smoking wood chips
  (cherry or apple)

Type of BBQ
Gas, pellet, charcoal, kamado,
  smoker

Makes
4 servings

Ingredients
Trout
½ cup (120 ml) bourbon
9 ounces (250 g) smoked trout
  or salmon
3 tablespoons maple syrup
Filling
5 ounces (150 g) cream cheese,
  such as Philadelphia, softened
1 tablespoon smoked paprika
½ tablespoon red pepper flakes
1 tablespoon kaffir lime oil or
  lemon-infused olive oil
1 red onion, finely diced
1 tablespoon chopped parsley
1 tablespoon chopped chives
Juice of 1 lime

Fill a large container with the bourbon and 4 cups (1 liter) of water. Add the cedar plank (plus a weight to keep it submerged) and let soak for 4 hours.

Preheat the BBQ and remove the cedar plank from the water. Moisten the wood chips slightly. Allow the BBQ temperature to decrease, then place the wood chips over the coals.

Brush the trout slices with the maple syrup (to lock in flavor from the smoke) and lay them on the cedar plank.

Place the plank on the grill over indirect heat and cook for 15 minutes. Allow to cool.

In a mixing bowl, combine the cream cheese, paprika, red pepper flakes, oil, onion, parsley, chives, and lime juice. Place a spoonful of the filling in the center of each trout slice, fold, and secure with a toothpick.

Tip from BIG T

A small glass of chardonnay or well-chilled champagne and you're all set!

BACON-WRAPPED STUFFED
MINI PEPPERS

Preparation Time: 25 minutes
Cooking Time: 25 minutes
Cooking Type: Direct + indirect heat

Equipment
Smoking box

Type of BBQ
Gas, pellet, charcoal, kamado, smoker

Makes
4 servings

Ingredients
10 piquillo peppers or mini bell peppers
20 slices smoked bacon
7 ½ ounces (225 g) cream cheese, such as Philadelphia, softened
2 red onions, minced
1 bunch parsley, chopped
1 tablespoon red pepper flakes (optional)
2 tablespoons maple syrup

Preheat the BBQ. Slice the piquillo peppers in half, keeping the stems intact. Remove the seeds.

Grill 10 slices of bacon until crisp, then chop finely.

In a mixing bowl, combine the cream cheese, red onions, chopped parsley, red pepper flakes, and chopped bacon. Mix well.

Stuff each pepper with the cream cheese mixture. Brush the remaining bacon slices with the maple syrup, then wrap each pepper with a slice of bacon. Secure with toothpicks if necessary.

Grill the peppers over direct heat until caramelized on both sides, then cook over indirect heat for 20 minutes.

CHICKEN TACOS
WITH CHEDDAR CREAM

Preparation Time: 15 minutes
Cooking Time: 25 minutes
Cooking Type: Direct + indirect heat

Equipment
Cast iron skillet

Type of BBQ
Gas, pellet, charcoal, kamado,
  smoker, brazier

Makes
4 servings

Ingredients
2 boneless skinless chicken breasts
Juice of 1 lime
1 tablespoon BBQ Dry Rub
  (see page 257)
3 tablespoons maple syrup
1 garlic clove, minced
1 small red chile pepper, minced
1 tablespoon neutral oil
1 red onion, diced
5 ounces (150 g) aged cheddar
  cheese, grated
2 cups (500 ml) heavy cream
1½ ounces (50 ml) bourbon
4 flour tortillas
2 sprigs parsley, chopped,
  for garnish
2 scallions, chopped, for garnish
Lime wedges, for serving

Score the chicken breasts shallowly. In a small bowl, combine the lime juice, dry rub, maple syrup, garlic, and chile pepper. Pour into a large resealable bag and add the chicken breasts. Seal the bag and turn to coat the chicken. Let marinate for 1 hour in the refrigerator.

Preheat the BBQ. Remove the chicken from the bag and grill over direct heat for 2 minutes per side, then move to indirect heat and cook for 10 minutes per side. Remove from the grill and keep warm.

Add the oil to the cast iron skillet. Place on the grill over direct heat and add the onions. Sauté until browned, then add the heavy cream and bourbon. Stir in the cheddar until smooth and creamy. Remove from the heat.

Grill the tortillas for 1 minute per side. Cut the chicken breasts into strips.

Spoon ¼ of the cheddar cream and ¼ of the chicken onto each tortilla. Garnish with parsley and scallions and serve with a lime wedge.

BAKED CHEESE
WITH CARAMELIZED WALNUTS

Preparation Time: 35 minutes
Cooking Time: 25–35 minutes
Cooking Type: Direct heat

Equipment
Cast iron skillet, aluminum foil

Type of BBQ
Gas, pellet, charcoal, kamado,
  smoker, brazier

Makes
4 servings

Ingredients
1 shallot, chopped
½ cup (120 ml) bourbon
2 ounces (60 g) walnut halves
1 tablespoon maple syrup
1 red onion, diced
1 round Vacherin Mont d'Or or
  Brie cheese (in its box)
¼ cup (60 ml) white wine
4 thick slices country bread

Preheat the BBQ. In a small bowl, combine the shallots and bourbon.

Place the cast iron skillet on the grill over direct heat. Add the walnuts, maple syrup, and onion and cook, stirring, until caramelized. Remove from heat and set aside.

Take the lid off the cheese box, then wrap the box in aluminum foil to prevent burning. Before you completely enclose the box, pour the wine between the box and the foil. Cut a slit in the top of the cheese and pour in the bourbon-shallot mixture. Close the foil.

Place the foil-wrapped cheese in the center of the coals. Close the BBQ lid and cook for 20–30 minutes, depending on your desired texture, stirring the cheese mixture halfway through.

Cut the bread into cubes. Pour the caramelized walnuts and onions over the cheese and serve with the bread for dipping.

Tip from BIG T

Adding wine to the aluminum foil will enhance the pine flavor from the box and create aromatic steam that will soak into the cheese.

TRANSCENDENT HOT AND COLD
OYSTERS

Preparation Time: 15 minutes
Cooking Time: 10 minutes
Cooking Type: Direct + indirect heat

Type of BBQ
Gas, pellet, charcoal, kamado, smoker, brazier

Makes
6 servings

Ingredients
12 oysters
Cold preparation
½ cup (120 ml) gin
1 teaspoon Worcestershire sauce
1 scallion, finely chopped
Juice of 1 lime
½ cup (120 ml) white balsamic vinegar
Pickled Red Onions (see page 258), for garnish
Hot preparation
Olive oil
1 shallot, minced
½ cup (120 ml) bourbon
¾ cup (180 ml) heavy cream
3 ½ ounces (100 g) hard cheese (such as Abondance or Comté), grated
A few fried onions, for garnish
Coarse salt, for serving

Preheat the BBQ.

Cold topping: In a medium bowl, combine the gin, Worcestershire sauce, scallion, lime juice, and balsamic vinegar. Place 6 oysters (rounded side down) on the grill over direct heat; they will open slightly in about 5 minutes. Transfer to a plate and remove the top shells. Divide the gin mixture between the oysters. Chill in the refrigerator.

Hot topping: In a small saucepan, warm a little olive oil and sauté the shallot until browned. Pour in the bourbon and flambé. Add the cream and grated cheese. Stir until smooth and keep warm.

Place the remaining 6 oysters (rounded side down) on the grill over direct heat; they will open slightly in about 5 minutes. Transfer to a plate and remove the top shells. Divide the bourbon mixture between the oysters.

Pour a layer of coarse salt onto a serving plate. Arrange the hot and cold oysters on the plate, nestling them in the salt. Top the cold oysters with pickled red onions and the hot oysters with fried onions. Serve immediately.

CAJUN CRAWFISH
WITH SPICY SAUCE

Preparation Time: 25 minutes
Cooking Time: 15 minutes
Cooking Type: Direct heat

Equipment
Large cast iron skillet

Type of BBQ
Gas, pellet, charcoal, kamado,
  smoker, brazier

Makes
6 servings

Ingredients
Olive oil
10 garlic cloves, thinly sliced
1 yellow onion, thinly sliced
2 celery stalks, cut into ½-inch
  (2-cm) pieces
½ cup (125 g) canned corn
1 pound (500 g) crawfish (or large
  shrimp, peeled and deveined,
  with tails on)
2 tablespoons cayenne pepper
  or 4 tablespoons Ginger & Lime
  Dry Rub (see page 257)
Kosher salt and freshly ground
  black pepper
¾ cup (180 ml) white wine
4 scallions, thinly sliced
1 bunch parsley, chopped
¾ cup (180 g) heavy cream
Cajun Rice (see p. 244), for serving

Preheat the BBQ.

Place the cast iron skillet on the grill over direct heat and add a drizzle of olive oil. Add the garlic, onion, celery, and corn, and sauté for about 5 minutes, until tender.

Add the crawfish, cayenne, salt and pepper to taste, and the white wine. Cook, stirring, for about 5 minutes, until the crawfish turn bright red and are fully cooked.

Remove the skillet from the heat and stir in the scallions, parsley, and cream.

Serve the crawfish with the Cajun rice.

SMOKED BBQ
POPCORN

Preparation Time: 15 minutes
Cooking Time: 8 minutes
Cooking Type: Direct heat

Equipment
Cast iron pot with lid

Type of BBQ
Gas, pellet, charcoal, kamado,
  smoker, brazier

Makes
6 servings

Ingredients
2 tablespoons coconut oil
½ cup (90 g) popcorn kernels
½ cup (120 g) unsalted butter,
  melted
2 tablespoons BBQ Dry Rub
  (see page 257)
1 teaspoon lemon pepper or freshly
  ground black pepper
1 teaspoon kosher salt

Preheat the BBQ.

Add the coconut oil to the cast iron pot and place it on the grill over direct heat. Add a few popcorn kernels to the pot. When they pop, add the remaining popcorn kernels, stir, and cover. Remove the pot from the heat once all the kernels have popped.

Pour the butter into the pot and stir to distribute it evenly.

In a large bowl, combine the dry rub, lemon pepper, and salt. Pour the popcorn into the bowl and toss to coat.

Let cool before serving. Store in an airtight container for up to 4 days.

Tip from BIG T

Coconut oil (or avocado oil) is ideal for high-heat cooking, as it has a high smoke point so it won't burn.

COLD-SMOKED
CHEESE BOARD

Preparation Time: 1 hour
Smoking Time: 2 hours
Cooking Type: Indirect heat

Equipment
Cedar plank, smoking box

Type of BBQ
Gas, pellet, charcoal, kamado,
 smoker

Makes
6 servings

Ingredients
½ cup (120 ml) white wine
1 round Reblochon cheese
 (or Brie or Camembert)
1 block cheddar cheese
 with hot peppers
1 round cow's milk Tomme cheese
 (or Gruyère)
Toasted bread, for serving

Note
Both firm cheeses (like Comté,
Beaufort, Parmesan) and soft-
rind cheeses (like Camembert,
Coulommiers, Brie, Muenster)
are good for smoking.

Fill a large container with the white wine and 4 cups (1 liter) of water. Add the cedar plank (plus a weight to keep it submerged) and let soak for at least 1 hour.

Prepare the BBQ for cold smoking at 68°F–86°F (20°C–30°C). Place the plank on the grill over indirect heat. Arrange the cheeses directly on the plank. The moisture from the wood will evaporate and create fragrant smoke. Let the cheese smoke for at least 2 hours.

Serve with toasted slices of bread.

Tip from BIG T

The cedar plank can be flavored according to your taste and creativity: bourbon, rum, cognac. Use the same amount as you would white wine.

STARTERS

GRILLED AVOCADO
WITH ROASTED OCTOPUS

Preparation Time: 1 hour 15 minutes
Cooking Time: 5 minutes
Cooking Method: Direct + indirect heat

Equipment
Griddle or grill plate, or cast iron skillet

Type of BBQ
Gas, pellet, charcoal, kamado, smoker, brazier

Serves
4 people

Ingredients
1 pound (500 g) octopus
1 onion, peeled and quartered
A few sprigs thyme
2 ripe avocados
½ lemon
Olive oil
Juice of 1 lime
3 ½ ounces (100 g) mayonnaise
1 spring onion, minced
4 garlic cloves, minced
1 bunch parsley, minced
Kosher salt and freshly ground pepper

Place the octopus in a large pot and cover it with water. Add the onion and thyme, bring to a boil, and then reduce heat to a simmer. Cook for 1 hour, then let the octopus cool in the cooking water.

Preheat the BBQ. Dry the octopus and grill it over direct heat for 1 minute on each side. Cut the octopus into small pieces, separating each tentacle. Let cool.

Cut the avocados in half, remove the pits, and squeeze the ½ lemon over the flesh to prevent oxidation. Score the avocado flesh with a knife in a cross-hatch pattern (don't pierce the skin).

Place the griddle or grill plate on the grill over indirect heat. Drizzle with a little olive oil and place the avocados flesh-side down until they get some color.

In a large bowl, combine the octopus, lime juice, mayonnaise, onion, garlic, and parsley. Season with salt and pepper to taste.

Divide the octopus mixture between the grilled avocado halves and serve.

GRILLED FRISÉE SALAD
WITH SMOKED BACON

Preparation Time: 15 minutes
Smoking Time: 3 hours
Cooking Time: 40 seconds
Cooking Method: Direct heat

Equipment
Smoking box, smoking wood chips
  (cherry), food processor

Type of BBQ
Gas, pellet, charcoal, kamado,
  smoker, brazier

Serves
4 people

Ingredients
1 head frisée (or escarole)
5 ⅓ ounces (150 g) thick-cut bacon
1 teaspoon maple syrup
2 garlic cloves, peeled
1 bunch parsley
¾ cup (200 ml) olive oil

Wash and separate the frisée leaves and set aside.

Prepare the smoking box with cherry wood chips. Place the bacon on the grill, brush it with the maple syrup, and smoke for 3 hours at 113°F (45°C). Let cool, then cut into thin strips.

In the bowl of the food processor, combine the garlic, parsley, and olive oil and puree until smooth. Brush the frisée leaves with some of the oil mixture, and set the rest aside.

Place the frisée leaves on the grill over direct heat for 40 seconds. Remove and let cool.

Arrange the frisée on a serving plate. Top with the smoked bacon and drizzle with the remaining olive oil mixture.

Tip from BIG T

For more flavors, add hard-boiled eggs and garlic-rubbed croutons to the salad.

GASPARD'S
PADRÓN PEPPERS

Preparation Time: 10 minutes
Cooking Time: 10 minutes
Resting Time: 4 hours
Cooking Method: Indirect heat

Equipment
Cast iron wok or pot, food processor

Type of BBQ
Gas, pellet, charcoal, kamado,
  smoker, brazier

Serves
4 people

Ingredients
20 Padrón peppers
¼ cup (50 ml) olive oil, plus more
  for finishing
Scant ½ cup (100 ml) maple syrup
10 garlic cloves, peeled
1 tablespoon Cajun seasoning
1 tablespoon smoked paprika
Kosher salt
½ lemon, for finishing
Balsamic vinegar, for finishing

Preheat the BBQ.

Place the wok on the grill, pour in the olive oil and maple syrup, add the garlic, and stir well until the oil is hot. Add the Padrón peppers, ensuring a good sizzle! Shake the wok to mix the flavors and caramelize everything. When peppers are well charred, add the Cajun seasoning and smoked paprika, stirring to coat everything evenly with the seasoning.

Remove the wok from the heat and let cool. Fish out 4 of the garlic cloves and add to the bowl of the food processor. Add a glug of olive oil and salt to taste, and blend until smooth. Let mixture rest for 4 hours.

Arrange the grilled peppers on a serving platter. Drizzle with the garlic-infused oil, a squeeze of lemon juice, and balsamic vinegar.

PAPI PAT'S
RUSTIC TOAST

Preparation Time: 15 minutes
Cooking Time: 1 hour 45 minutes
Cooking Method: Direct +
indirect heat

Equipment
Cast iron skillet

Type of BBQ
Gas, pellet, charcoal, kamado,
  smoker

Serves
4 people

Ingredients
1 Morteau sausage (or Montbéliard
  sausage or diot Savoyard)
1 scant cup (200 ml) white wine
Olive oil
4 red onions, peeled and thickly
  sliced
4 garlic cloves, sliced
2 sprigs thyme
2 tablespoons unsalted butter,
  at room temperature
4 thick slices country bread
1 round Reblochon cheese

Preheat the BBQ.

Place the cast iron skillet on the grill over direct heat. Add the sausage
and pour in the wine. Bring to a boil and cook for 45 minutes. Remove the
sausage and set aside to cool.

In the same skillet over direct heat, warm a drizzle of olive oil and add the
onions, garlic, and thyme. Cook until the vegetables begin to caramelize,
then cover the skillet with aluminum foil and move to indirect heat
for 45 minutes.

Transfer the vegetables to a bowl and add the butter. Mix to combine.
Spread the butter on the slices of country bread, then grill the bread,
butter side up, until the butter melts.

Arrange slices of Reblochon, slices of sausage, and caramelized onions
on each piece of bread. Place back on the grill over indirect heat until
the cheese melts.

GRILLED LEEK
TARTINE

Preparation Time: 15 minutes
Cooking Time: 20 minutes
Marinade: 30 minutes
Cooking Method: Direct heat

Type of BBQ
Gas, pellet, charcoal, kamado,
   smoker, brazier

Serves
4 people

Ingredients
4 leeks
5 ounces (150 g) fresh cheese,
   like St. Môret or mozzarella,
   or cream cheese
Juice of 2 lemons, divided
1 bunch chives, finely chopped
1 bunch parsley, finely chopped
2 red onions, thinly sliced
3 tablespoons olive oil
2 tablespoons soy sauce
2 thick slices country bread

Preheat the BBQ.

Rinse and dry the leeks, then place them whole in the coals and
cook until the skin turns black, about 15 minutes.

In a medium bowl, combine the cheese, juice of 1 lemon, chives, parsley,
and onions and stir to mix. Cover and reserve in the fridge.

Remove the charred leeks from the coals and let cool. Discard the tops
and outer layers, reserving the tender hearts. Slice the leeks thinly.
In a medium bowl, combine the leeks with the olive oil, soy sauce, and
remaining lemon juice. Let marinate for 30 minutes.

Place the country bread on the grill until charred. Remove from the grill
and spread with the cheese mixture. Top with the marinated leeks.
Cut each piece of bread in two to make 4 servings.

Tip from BIG T

For more umami, grate a little Parmesan over the tartines before serving.

BIG T'S
CLUB SANDWICH

Preparation Time: 25 minutes
Cooking Time: 25 minutes
Cooking Method: Indirect heat

Type of BBQ
Gas, pellet, charcoal, kamado,
  brazier

Serves
4 people

Ingredients
4 large eggs
4 boneless skinless chicken breasts
4 tablespoons Chicken Dry Rub
  (see page 256)
8 slices smoked bacon
3 tablespoons unsalted butter,
  at room temperature
12 slices white bread
8 pickles (or Pickled Mango,
  see page 258)
8 lettuce leaves
Curry Mayonnaise
1 large egg yolk
1 tablespoon Dijon mustard
1 tablespoon Madras curry powder
Fleur de sel and freshly ground
  black pepper
1 cup (225 ml) sunflower oil
6 chives, minced
4 garlic cloves, minced

Bring a saucepan of water to a boil, then add the eggs and boil for
10 minutes. Remove the hard-boiled eggs from the water, cool them
in an ice-water bath, and peel them.

Butterfly the chicken breasts (cut horizontally into the thickest part of
each breast, then open it like a book) and season all over with the dry rub.
Place the chicken breasts on the grill over indirect heat and cook for
10 minutes on each side. Grill the bacon as well.

Spread the butter on one side of each slice of bread and lightly toast
the bread on the grill, buttered side up.

Make the curry mayonnaise: In a large bowl, whisk together the egg yolk,
mustard, curry powder, and fleur de sel and pepper to taste. Whisking
continuously, slowly and gradually add the oil until the mixture emulsifies.
Stir in the chopped garlic and chives.

Chop the hard-boiled eggs and mix them with half of the mayonnaise
in a bowl. Set the rest of the mayonnaise aside.

Cut the chicken breasts into pieces that will fit the bread. If desired,
cut the bacon, slice the pickles, and chop the lettuce.

Spread the curry mayonnaise on the buttered side of each slice of bread.
Add chicken, pickles, lettuce, and bacon. Cover with a second slice of
bread. Spread the egg mayonnaise mixture on top, repeat fillings,
and close with a third slice of bread.

Secure each sandwich with toothpicks and cut in half diagonally
to create triangles.

Tip from BIG T

Swap the chicken for smoked salmon or turkey breast.

ROASTED TOMATO SALAD
WITH CONFIT GARLIC AND SMOKED FETA

Preparation Time: 25 minutes
Cooking Time: 1 hour
Smoking Time: 1 hour
Cooking Method: Indirect heat

Equipment
Cedar plank, smoking box, 2 cast
  iron skillets

Type of BBQ
Gas, pellet, charcoal, kamado,
  smoker, brazier

Serves
4 people

Ingredients
5 ⅓ ounces (150 g) feta
20 garlic cloves, unpeeled
Olive oil
Coarse salt
10 ounces (280 g) cherry tomatoes
3 sprigs thyme
4 sprigs rosemary
Fleur de sel
2 red onions, sliced
2 tablespoons white balsamic
  vinegar
A few basil leaves, chopped
4 chives, chopped
4 sprigs parsley, chopped
Freshly ground black pepper

Place the feta on a cedar plank and smoke it over indirect heat at 86°F (30°C) for 1 hour.

Place the garlic cloves in one cast iron skillet, cover with olive oil, and add a pinch of coarse salt. Cover the skillet with aluminum foil and cook over indirect heat for 1 hour.

While the garlic cooks, place the cherry tomatoes in the second cast iron skillet, and add the thyme and rosemary. Drizzle with olive oil and sprinkle with fleur de sel. Cover the skillet with aluminum foil and place in the center of the grill. Cook for 12 to 15 minutes, until the tomatoes are tender and juicy. Remove the thyme and rosemary.

On a plate, arrange the roasted tomatoes, onion slices, crumbled smoked feta, and confit garlic cloves. Drizzle with olive oil and the white balsamic vinegar. Garnish with chopped basil, chives, and parsley. Season with pepper to taste.

Variation with Confit Peaches

Replace the confit garlic with confit peaches: Cut 8 peaches in half and remove the pits. In a cast iron skillet, melt 1 ½ tablespoons unsalted butter. When the butter foams, add the peach halves and brown them. Add 6 tablespoons lavender honey, 1 cup (225 ml) water, and 4 tablespoons maple syrup. Cover with aluminum foil and cook over indirect heat for 1 hour.

VEGETARIAN TACOS
WITH GRILLED CORN

Preparation Time: 15 minutes
Cooking Time: 12 minutes
Cooking Method: Direct heat

Equipment
Cast iron saucepan

Type of BBQ
Gas, pellet, charcoal, kamado,
 smoker, brazier

Serves
4 people

Ingredients
1½ tablespoons unsalted butter
¼ cup (50 ml) citrus-infused oil
 or another flavored oil
2 sprigs parsley, chopped
4 ears of corn, husks removed
8 small flour tortillas
½ cup Pickled Red Onions
 (see page 258)
Juice of 1 lime
1 tablespoon BBQ Dry Rub
 (see page 257)
3 tablespoons maple syrup
1 garlic clove, minced
1 red chile pepper, thinly sliced

Preheat the BBQ. Clean and oil the grill.

In the cast iron saucepan, combine the butter, citrus oil, and chopped parsley, and heat until melted.

Brush the corn cobs with the melted butter mixture and place them directly on the grill. Grill for 10 minutes, turning every 2 minutes, until corn is evenly colored on all sides.

Grill the tortillas on the oiled grill grates for 1 minute on each side.

Using a knife, cut the kernels off the cobs into a bowl. Add the pickled red onions, lime juice, dry rub, maple syrup, garlic, and chile pepper. Mix well.

Spoon the corn mixture onto the grilled tortillas and serve.

BAGUETTE
PIZZA

Preparation Time: 30 minutes
Cooking Time: 40 minutes
Marinade Time: 15 minutes
**Cooking Method: Direct +
indirect heat**

Equipment
Cast iron saucepan, aluminum foil

Type of BBQ
Gas, pellet, charcoal, kamado,
  smoker, brazier

Serves
4 people

Ingredients
1 garlic head
Olive oil
1 red onion, sliced thickly
3 medium tomatoes
2 tablespoons crème fraîche
1 green bell pepper, diced
1 yellow bell pepper, diced
2 tablespoons sweet soy sauce
Leaves from 1 sprig thyme
Espelette pepper
Kosher salt and freshly ground
  black pepper
1 baguette
5 ounces (150 g) grated Gruyère
  or smoked mozzarella
Chopped parsley

Preheat the BBQ. Slice ¼ to ½ inch off the top of the head of garlic to expose the cloves. Drizzle with olive oil and wrap the garlic in aluminum foil. Place the onions in another piece of aluminum foil, and place both packets on the grill over indirect heat for 45 minutes, until softened. Set aside to cool.

Bring a medium pot of water to a boil. With the tip of a knife, make a small X on the base of each tomato. Lower the tomatoes into the boiling water for 30 seconds and remove them with a slotted spoon. Let cool slightly, then peel and chop the tomatoes. In a medium bowl, combine the tomatoes and crème fraîche.

In a medium bowl, combine the diced peppers and soy sauce and let marinate for 15 minutes.

Place the cast iron saucepan on the grill over direct heat and add the peppers. Cook for 15 minutes until charred and softened.

Unwrap the onion and garlic packets. Squeeze the garlic cloves into a medium bowl, and add the onions, tomato mixture, thyme leaves, and a pinch of Espelette pepper. Mix well and season with salt and pepper to taste.

Cut the baguette lengthwise and spread each side with the garlic mixture. Sprinkle each baguette with the grated cheese. Place the baguette halves on the grill over indirect heat until warmed through and cheese is melted.

Sprinkle with parsley, cut into pieces, and serve.

Variation

Add spicy sausage, cooked ground meat, shredded chicken, or canned tuna to the filling.

MUSHROOM
SOUP

Preparation Time: 25 minutes
Cooking Time: 45 minutes
Cooking Method: Direct + indirect heat

Equipment
Cast iron saucepan, immersion blender

Type of BBQ
Gas, pellet, charcoal, kamado, brazier

Serves
2 people

Ingredients
2 round country bread loaves (about 14 ounces/400 g each)
2 tablespoons olive oil (or truffle oil), plus more for finishing
2 tablespoons unsalted butter
1 garlic clove, chopped
2 onions, chopped
1 pound (450 g) button mushrooms, cleaned and cut into quarters
1 tablespoon all-purpose flour
¼ cup (60 ml) white wine
Kosher salt and freshly ground black pepper
4 cups (1 liter) chicken broth
½ ounce (14 g) dried mushrooms of your choice
¼ cup (60 ml) crème fraîche (35% fat)
2 tablespoons chopped parsley, for garnish
1 tablespoon chopped chives, for garnish
2 tablespoons fried onions, for garnish

Preheat the BBQ.

Make 2 bread bowls: Cut off the tops of the loaves and set aside. Scoop out much of the inside of the bread and reserve for another use. Drizzle 1 tablespoon of olive oil inside each hollowed loaf. Place the loaves (without the tops) on the grill over indirect heat, and cook for 15 to 20 minutes to harden the crust. Set aside.

Place the cast iron saucepan on the grill over direct heat. Add the butter and then the garlic and onions. Sauté for a few minutes, and then add mushrooms (hold a few back for garnish). Sauté until browned, stirring regularly.

Sprinkle the flour over the mushrooms and cook, stirring, for 1 minute. Deglaze with the white wine and let it reduce. Season with salt and pepper to taste. Add the chicken broth and dried mushrooms. Bring to a boil, then reduce to a simmer and cook for 20 minutes, stirring occasionally.

With the immersion blender, puree the soup until smooth, then stir in the crème fraîche. Taste and adjust seasonings.

Ladle the soup into the hollowed bread loaves. Garnish with the reserved mushrooms, the chopped chives and parsley, and a drizzle of olive or truffle oil. Sprinkle with fried onions and serve.

SMOKED
DEVILED EGGS

Preparation Time: 15 minutes
Soaking Time: 30 minutes
Smoking Time: 15 minutes
Cooking Method: Indirect heat

Equipment

Cast iron saucepan, smoking box,
5 ⅓ ounces (150 g) smoking wood
chips, soaked for 30 minutes and
drained

Type of BBQ

Gas, pellet, charcoal, kamado,
smoker

Serves

4 people

Ingredients

12 large eggs
1 tablespoon Butcher Blend spice
  mix (see page 256)
5 ⅓ ounces (150 g) mayonnaise
¼ teaspoon Worcestershire sauce
¼ teaspoon Tabasco sauce
Kosher salt and freshly ground
  pepper
Chopped chives, for garnish
Chopped parsley, for garnish

Fill the cast iron saucepan with water and place on the grill over
direct heat. Bring to a boil, then add the eggs and boil for 10 minutes.
Remove the hard-boiled eggs from the water, cool them in an ice-water
bath, and peel them.

Place the eggs on the grill over indirect heat, close the lid, and smoke
for 15 minutes. Remove the eggs carefully and allow them to cool to
room temperature.

Cut the cooled eggs in half. Scoop out the yolks with a spoon and place
them in a medium bowl. Add the spice mix, mayonnaise, Worcestershire
sauce, and Tabasco sauce. Season with salt and pepper to taste and mix
until smooth.

Spoon the yolk mixture into the egg whites. Garnish with chopped chives
and parsley, then serve.

GRILLED AVOCADO TOAST
WITH MARINATED MUSHROOMS

Preparation Time: 25 minutes
Marinade Time: 30 minutes
Cooking Time: 15 minutes
**Cooking Method: Direct +
indirect heat**

Equipment
Griddle or grill plate

Type of BBQ
Gas, pellet, charcoal, kamado,
  smoker, brazier

Serves
4 people

Ingredients
1 pound (500 g) button mushrooms
Juice of 2 limes, divided
2 tablespoons soy sauce
4 avocados
Citrus-infused olive oil
1 red onion, thinly sliced
1 habanero pepper, minced
2 bunches chives, chopped
Kosher salt and freshly ground
  black pepper
4 thick slices country bread
5 ⅓ ounces (150 g) ricotta
  or softened cream cheese

Clean the mushrooms and use a mandoline to slice them thinly.
In a large bowl, combine the mushrooms, juice from 1 lime, and soy
sauce. Marinate for 30 minutes at room temperature.

Place the griddle or grill plate on the grill over indirect heat and brush
with a drizzle of the olive oil. Cut the avocados in half and remove the pits.
Place the avocados on the plate flesh-side down and grill until they char.
Let cool to room temperature.

In a medium bowl, combine the avocado with the remaining lime juice
and the onion, habanero, chives, 2 tablespoons of the citrus-infused olive
oil, and salt and pepper to taste.

Grill the slices of country bread on the BBQ. Spread each slice
with cheese, then top with the avocado mixture and the marinated
mushrooms. Serve immediately.

MEAT

COOKING

GUIDE

RIBEYE STEAK

Preparation Time: 10 minutes
Cooking Time: 24 minutes
Cooking Method: Direct + indirect heat

Equipment
Meat press or cast iron skillet, meat thermometer

Type of BBQ
Gas, pellet, charcoal, kamado, smoker

Makes
4 servings

Ingredients
1 tomahawk or cowboy steak (bone-in ribeye), up to 3 ¼ pounds (1.5 kg)
¼ cup (50 g) Butcher Blend spice mix (see page 256)
Olive oil

Remove the meat from the refrigerator 2 hours before cooking to bring it to room temperature.

Preheat the BBQ. Clean and oil the grill.

In a bowl, combine the spice mix with just enough olive oil to create a sandy paste. Rub this mixture onto the steak, pressing firmly to ensure the spices penetrate the meat.

Place the steak on the very hot grill over direct heat. Place the meat press or cast iron skillet on top of the steak. Grill for 4 minutes on each side to create a Maillard reaction, forming a crust that locks in flavor and juices, while giving the steak a beautiful caramelization.

After searing, move the steak to indirect heat, close the grill lid, and cook for 8 minutes on each side.

Use the meat thermometer to check the internal temperature for perfect doneness (see the guide on page 27). Let rest for 15 minutes before serving.

IMPORTANT

Avoid piercing the meat with a fork to prevent juice loss.

HANGER STEAK
WITH SHALLOTS & CONFIT GARLIC

Preparation Time: 15 minutes
Cooking Time: 10 minutes
**Cooking Method: Direct +
indirect heat**

Equipment
2 cast iron saucepans

Type of BBQ
Gas, pellet, charcoal, kamado,
  smoker

Makes
4 servings

Ingredients
1 pound (500 g) hanger steak
2 cups (500 ml) peanut oil
4 shallots, finely chopped
4 garlic cloves, unpeeled
1 ½ tablespoons (10 g) unsalted
  butter
2 teaspoons (5 g) all-purpose flour
1 beef bouillon cube
Scant ½ cup (100 ml) red wine
  or port
¼ cup (30 g) Butcher Blend spice
  mix (see page 258)
Olive oil

Remove the meat from the refrigerator 2 hours before cooking to bring
it to room temperature.

Preheat the BBQ.

Place one of the cast iron saucepans on the grill over indirect heat and
add the peanut oil. Once the oil is hot, add the shallots, and fry until
golden. Remove with a slotted spoon or mesh strainer and transfer to
paper towels to drain. Add the garlic cloves and fry until garlic is softened.
Remove to paper towels.

Place the other saucepan over direct heat and add the butter. When it
melts, stir in the flour and whisk to form a roux. Add the bouillon cube,
about half the fried shallots and half the garlic (squeeze it out of the peel),
and mix well. Move the pan to indirect heat, stir in the wine or port, and let
it reduce by half.

In a bowl, combine the spice mix with just enough olive oil to create a
sandy paste. Rub this mixture onto the steak, pressing firmly to ensure
the spices penetrate the meat.

Place the steak on the grill over direct heat and cook 3–4 minutes on
each side for medium-rare. Adjust cooking time for desired doneness.

Remove the steak from the grill and let it rest for 5 minutes. Slice against
the grain and serve with the top with the remaining shallots, confit
garlic, and sauce.

BEEF
SHORT RIBS

Preparation Time: 20 minutes
Cooking Time: 6 hours
Cooking Method: Indirect heat

Equipment
Smoker, meat thermometer,
  butcher paper (or aluminum foil)

Type of BBQ
Gas, pellet, charcoal, kamado,
  smoker

Makes
4 servings

Ingredients
4 beef short ribs, white membrane
  removed
¼ cup (50 g) BBQ Dry Rub
  (see page 257)
¾ cup (200 ml) "Got You Babe" BBQ
  Sauce (see page 252)

Preheat the smoker to 225°F (107°C). While it heats, coat the short ribs with the dry rub, ensuring even coverage.

Place the ribs in the smoker and cook for 5 hours, or until the internal temperature reaches 205°F (96°C). A nice crust should form on the outside and the interior should be quite tender.

Remove the ribs from the smoker and brush them generously with the BBQ sauce. Wrap them in butcher paper.

Lower the smoker temperature to 200°F (93°C). Return the ribs to the smoker for another hour to allow the sauce to caramelize and the ribs to tenderize further.

Remove from the smoker, unwrap, and serve.

Tip from BIG T

Among the best storebought BBQ sauces, I highly recommend the one from Maison Martin—it's exceptional.

BRAISED BEEF CHEEKS
IN RED WINE SAUCE

Preparation Time: 20 minutes
Cooking Time: 3 hours
Cooking Method: Indirect heat

Equipment
Cast iron Dutch oven

Type of BBQ
Gas, pellet, charcoal, kamado,
   smoker

Makes
6 servings

Ingredients
¼ cup (60 ml) olive oil
5 ½ tablespoons unsalted butter
3 pounds (1.3 kg) beef cheeks
Kosher salt and freshly ground
   black pepper
2 yellow onions, chopped
4 carrots, chopped
3 ½ ounces (100 g) mushrooms,
   chopped
5 ⅓ ounces (150 g) smoked bacon,
   diced
2 tablespoons maple syrup
1 ½ cups (330 ml) amber beer
4 cups (1 liter) beef or veal stock
¼ cup (60 ml) apple cider vinegar
1 sprig thyme
5 garlic cloves, peeled
½ cup (120 ml) red wine
Chopped chives, for garnish

Preheat the BBQ. Place the Dutch oven on the grill over indirect heat and add the olive oil and 3 ½ tablespoons of the butter. Season the beef cheeks with salt and pepper, and then sear for 5 minutes on each side. Remove and set aside.

To the Dutch oven, add the onions, carrots, mushrooms, and bacon. Stir to combine, then add the maple syrup and cook for 20 minutes until vegetables are caramelized. Add the beer and stir to deglaze.

Add the stock, vinegar, thyme, and garlic cloves. Return the beef cheeks to the pot, cover, and bring to a boil.

Move the Dutch oven to the center of the BBQ. Close the lid and cook for 2 ½ hours, or until the meat is tender.

Remove the thyme, beef cheeks, and vegetables from the pot. Reduce the sauce until thickened, then add the remaining 2 tablespoons butter and the red wine. Return the meat and vegetables to the pot, stir well, and adjust seasoning if needed. Garnish with chopped chives.

Tip from BIG T

This dish is delicious served with buttery mashed potatoes.

BEEF AND PEPPER
SKEWERS

Preparation Time: 15 minutes
Marinade Time: 6 hours
Rest Time: 2 hours
Cooking Time: 5 minutes
**Cooking Method: Direct +
indirect heat**

Type of BBQ
Gas, pellet, charcoal, kamado,
  smoker

Makes
4 servings

Ingredients
2 ¼ pounds (1 kg) rump heart
  or sirloin
2 tablespoons Butcher Blend spice
  mix (see page 256)
2 tablespoons smoked paprika
Juice of 1 lime
1 tablespoon Maggi seasoning
  or Worcestershire sauce
5 tablespoons maple syrup
½ cup (120 ml) olive oil
2 red bell peppers
2 green bell peppers
4 red onions

Cut the meat into 1 ½ -inch (4-cm) cubes. Place in a resealable bag
and add the spice mix, paprika, lime juice, Maggi seasoning, maple syrup,
and olive oil. Seal the bag and marinate in the refrigerator for 6 hours.

Cut the peppers and onions into squares the same size as
the meat cubes.

Thread the meat, peppers, and onions onto 4 skewers. Let them sit
at room temperature for 2 hours.

Preheat the BBQ. Clean and oil the grill.

Place the skewers on the grill over direct heat and cook for 2 minutes,
turning them once halfway through. Move them to indirect heat,
close the BBQ lid, and cook for 3 more minutes.

RIBEYE
IN BREAD CRUST

Preparation Time: 45 minutes
Rest Time: 2 hours
Cooking Time: 30 minutes
**Cooking Method: Direct +
indirect heat**

Equipment
Stand mixer

Type of BBQ
Gas, pellet, charcoal, kamado,
 smoker

Makes
4 servings

Ingredients
4 cups (500 g) all-purpose flour
1¼ cups (300 ml) warm water
2 (2¼ teaspoon) packets active
 dry yeast
1 teaspoon kosher salt
3 tablespoons neutral oil
2 tablespoons chopped thyme
1 tablespoon red pepper flakes
1 pound (500 g) ribeye steak
2 tablespoons Dijon mustard
1 large egg, beaten

In the bowl of the stand mixer fitted with the dough hook (or in a large bowl), combine the flour, water, yeast, salt, oil, thyme, and red pepper flakes. Knead until smooth, then cover the bowl with a clean cloth and let the dough rise for 1 hour at room temperature.

Preheat the BBQ.

Place the steak on the grill over direct heat and sear each side and the edges for 1 minute each. Remove steak from the grill and coat it on all sides with the mustard.

On a floured surface, roll out the dough into a large rectangle big enough to wrap around the steak. Place the ribeye in the center of the dough and fold it over to enclose the meat, sealing the edges with a little water. Brush the dough with the beaten egg. Let it rise for 1 hour at room temperature.

Preheat the BBQ again. Place the dough-wrapped steak on the grill over indirect heat. Put a container of water underneath to maintain moisture. Cook for 30 minutes, until the bread dough is golden brown.

Slice and serve immediately.

BIG T'S
BURGER

Preparation Time: 20 minutes
Cooking Time: 15 minutes
Cooking Method: Direct + indirect heat

Equipment

Cast iron skillet, burger cloche or aluminum foil

Type of BBQ

Gas, pellet, charcoal, kamado, smoker

Makes

4 servings

Ingredients

2 red onions, thinly sliced
3 tablespoons white balsamic vinegar
1 tablespoon unsalted butter
4 slices smoked bacon
1⅓ pounds (600 g) ground beef
Kosher salt
4 slices smoked raclette or cheddar
4 burger buns
¾ cup (180 ml) "Got You Babe" BBQ sauce (see page 252)
Dill pickle chips
Shredded iceberg lettuce

In a large bowl, combine the onions and vinegar and let them marinate for 2 hours.

Preheat the BBQ.

Place the cast iron skillet on the grill over direct heat. Add the butter and, when it melts, add the bacon slices. Cook until crisp and set aside to drain on paper towels. Move the skillet to indirect heat (don't drain the grease).

Shape the beef into 4 equal-sized balls, then flatten them into patties about ¾ inch (2 cm) thick. Salt the patties on both sides, then place them in the skillet over indirect heat. Cook, flipping a few times, until the internal temperature reaches 160°F (71°C).

A few minutes before the patties are cooked, place slices of cheese on the hot patties and cover with a burger dome or aluminum foil to allow the cheese to melt completely. Transfer the patties to a plate.

Add the buns to the skillet, cut side down, and toast in the juices left from cooking the meat.

Spread BBQ sauce on the bottom half of each toasted bun. To each bottom bun, add a slice of bacon, onions, pickles, a layer of lettuce, and a cheeseburger patty. Close with the top half of the bun.

Tip from BIG T

For burgers, it's important to choose meat with a higher fat content; it will be more flavorful and keep the burger tender.

GRANDMA'S
SHEPHERD'S PIE

Preparation Time: 30 minutes
Cooking Time: 4 hours 25 minutes
Cooking Method: Indirect heat

Equipment
Butcher paper, kitchen twine, cast iron Dutch oven

Type of BBQ
Gas, pellet, charcoal, kamado, smoker

Makes
4 servings

Ingredients
2 ¼ pounds (1 kg) pork belly
¾ cup (180 ml) maple syrup
1 yellow onion, quartered
4 garlic cloves, peeled
1 pound (500 g) Yukon Gold potatoes, peeled and cut into large chunks
4 cups (1 liter) milk
2 cups (500 ml) crème fraîche
¼ cup chopped parsley
2 ½ ounces (70 g) crusty day-old bread, cut into small cubes
1 ½ tablespoons unsalted butter, at room temperature
¾ cup (180 ml) white wine
3 ½ ounces (100 g) grated Beaufort cheese (or Gruyère)

Preheat the BBQ. Brush the pork belly on all sides with the maple syrup, and place on a piece of butcher paper large enough to enclose it. Top with the onions and garlic, and wrap up the paper around the pork and vegetables, securing with kitchen twine. Place on the grill over indirect heat and cook for 4 hours.

In a large saucepan, combine the milk and 4 cups (1 l) water. Add the potatoes and bring to a boil. Cook 25 minutes or until tender. Drain the potatoes and, in a large bowl, mash them with the cream and parsley.

Unwrap the pork belly, and add the onions and garlic to the bowl with the potatoes. Transfer the pork belly to a large bowl and shred it with a fork. Stir in the bread cubes and butter.

In the Dutch oven, spread half the mashed potatoes, then to with the pork mixture. Pour the white wine over the pork. Add the remaining mashed potatoes on top, then finish with the grated cheese.

Place the Dutch oven on the grill over indirect heat and cook for 25 minutes, until the top is golden brown.

Tip from BIG T

This recipe also works well with veal or beef chuck.

CARNIVORE
BURRITOS

Preparation Time: 20 minutes
Cooking Time: 45 minutes
Cooking Method: Indirect heat

Equipment
Cast iron skillet

Type of BBQ
Gas, pellet, charcoal, kamado,
  smoker

Makes
4 servings

Ingredients
Olive oil
2 bell peppers, seeded and sliced
1 yellow onion, sliced
1 red onion, sliced
4 garlic cloves, sliced
3 ½ ounces (100 g) canned corn
3 ½ tablespoons (50 g) unsalted
  butter
1 pound (500 g) ground beef
  (20% fat)
⅔ cup (150 ml) bourbon
⅔ cup (150 ml) beef broth
4 tablespoons Mexican spice mix
  or taco seasoning
½ bunch parsley, chopped
½ bunch cilantro, chopped
4 tortillas

Preheat the BBQ.

Place the cast iron skillet on the grill over indirect heat. Add a drizzle of olive oil. Add the peppers, onions, garlic, and corn, and sauté until caramelized. Transfer the vegetables to a bowl to cool, then return the skillet to indirect heat. Add butter and the ground beef and cook for 15 minutes. Add the bourbon and flambé, then add the beef broth and Mexican spice mix. Reduce until the liquid is absorbed, then stir in the sautéed vegetables and chopped herbs.

Spoon the mixture into tortillas, roll them up, and press down to seal. Grill the burritos over indirect heat for 1 minute on each side.

Tip from BIG T

Add about 3 ½ ounces (100 g) grated Monterey Jack or mozzarella to the mixture to give it a cheesier flavor.

STUFFED PEPPERS

Preparation Time: 20 minutes
Cooking Time: 1 hour
Cooking Method: Indirect heat

Equipment
Cast iron skillet

Type of BBQ
Gas, pellet, charcoal, kamado,
  smoker

Makes
4 servings

Ingredients
4 bell peppers
¾ cup (200 ml) crème fraîche
  or heavy cream
2 tablespoons (30 ml) Dijon
  mustard
¾ cup (200 ml) cognac
1 tablespoon Butcher Blend spice
  mix or Chicken Dry Rub
  (see page 256)
2 slices stale bread
3 tablespoons unsalted butter
1 pound (500 g) ground veal or beef
1 pound (500 g) ground pork
Kosher salt and freshly ground
  black pepper
2 yellow onions, chopped
4 garlic cloves, chopped
⅔ cup (150 ml) white wine
1 bunch parsley
Olive oil

Preheat the BBQ.

Slice the tops off the bell peppers horizontally (reserving the tops), and remove the seeds. If necessary, cut a thin slice off the bottoms of the peppers so they stand upright.

In a bowl, mix the crème fraîche, mustard, cognac, and spice mix. Add the bread and let soak for 10 minutes. Transfer to a blender and blend until smooth.

Place the cast iron skillet on the grill over indirect heat. Add the butter, and when it melts, add the ground veal and pork and salt and pepper to taste. Sauté until cooked through, then add the white wine, garlic, and onions, and cook until the wine mostly cooks off.

Let cool, then stir in the soaked bread. Stuff the peppers with the meat mixture, replace the pepper tops, and grill on indirect heat for 45 minutes.

Tip from BIG T

This recipe works well with tuna and potatoes: replace the ground meat with the same amount of canned tuna, and substitute the garlic cloves with about 30 Kalamata olives. Stuff into hollowed-out potato halves and grill.

COOKING GUIDE

PORK CHOP

Preparation Time: 15 minutes
Cooking Time: 25 minutes
Cooking Method: Direct + indirect heat

Equipment
Meat press or cast iron skillet, meat thermometer

Type of BBQ
Gas, pellet, charcoal, kamado, brazier

Makes
4 servings

Ingredients
2 ¼ pounds (1 kg) thick-cut, bone-in pork chop with fat cap on (ideally free-range/pastured)
2 tablespoons Butcher Blend spice mix (see page 256)
2 tablespoons smoked paprika
Olive oil

Note
Avoid grilling thinner pork chops, as their lack of fat causes them to dry out and toughen.

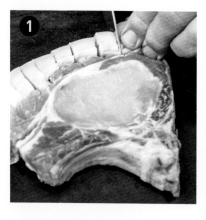

❶ Remove the meat from the refrigerator 2 hours before cooking to bring it to room temperature.

Preheat the BBQ.
Clean and oil the grill.

❷ Score the fat on the pork chop, leaving it attached to the meat. In a bowl, combine the spice mix and paprika with just enough olive oil to create a sandy paste. Rub this mixture onto the chop, pressing firmly to ensure the spices penetrate the meat.

❸ Place the chop on the grill over direct heat, then place the meat press or cast iron skillet on top. Grill for 5 minutes on each side.

Move the chop to indirect heat and cook for 15 minutes, turning halfway through.

TIP

Chef's option

Instead of cooking the pork chop directly on the grill, after you apply the seasoning to the meat, place a cast iron skillet on the grill over direct heat. Add 2 tablespoons of butter and 4 sprigs thyme. Once the butter is melted and foamy, add the pork chop and spoon butter continually over it. Cook for 15 minutes, flipping once halfway through. Check the internal temperature with the meat thermometer—it should reach 145°F (63°C).

PORK TENDERLOIN
WITH YOGURT SAUCE

Preparation Time: 20 minutes
Cooking Time: 3 hours
Cooking Method: Indirect heat

Equipment
Butcher paper, kitchen twine, meat
 thermometer

Type of BBQ
Gas, pellet, charcoal, kamado,
 smoker

Makes
4 servings

Ingredients
2 ¼ pounds (1 kg) pork tenderloin
4 tablespoons BBQ Dry Rub
 (see page 257)
Olive oil
2 tablespoons unsalted butter,
 cubed
Yogurt Sauce:
1 cup (250 g) Greek yogurt
⅓ cup (80 ml) white balsamic
 vinegar
½ bunch cilantro, chopped
½ bunch mint, chopped
½ bunch parsley, chopped
1 cucumber, seeded and diced
1 red onion, thinly sliced
10 garlic cloves, minced
10 Kalamata olives, chopped
2 tablespoons smoked paprika
Juice of 1 lime
Kosher salt and freshly ground
 black pepper

Preheat the BBQ.

In a bowl, combine the dry rub with just enough olive oil to create a sandy
paste. Rub this mixture onto the tenderloin, pressing firmly to ensure the
spices penetrate the meat.

Place the tenderloin on a large sheet of butcher paper, dot with butter,
wrap tightly, and tie with kitchen twine.

Place the wrapped tenderloin on the grill over indirect heat and cook
for 3 hours, or until the internal temperature reaches 145°F (63°C).

While pork cooks, in a large bowl, combine the yogurt, balsamic vinegar,
cilantro, mint, parsley, cucumber, onions, garlic, olives, paprika, and lime
juice in a large bowl. Mix and season with salt and pepper to taste.

Slice the tenderloin and serve with yogurt sauce.

BATON ROUGE-STYLE
RIBS

Preparation Time: 20 minutes
Cooking Time: 2 hours 15 minutes
Cooking Method: Direct + indirect heat

Equipment
Small cast iron pot, aluminum foil

Type of BBQ
Gas, pellet, charcoal, kamado, smoker

Makes
4 servings

Ingredients
1⅓ pounds (600 g) pork ribs, cut into 2 pieces
Neutral oil
1 teaspoon Louisiana spice mix or Texas rub
2 teaspoons smoked paprika
2 teaspoons onion powder
1 teaspoon garlic powder
1 teaspoon kosher salt
1 teaspoon freshly ground black pepper
12 ounces (350 ml) dark beer
1 cup (250 ml) ketchup
1 cup (250 ml) molasses
2 tablespoons brown sugar
2 tablespoons white vinegar

Preheat the BBQ. Place the ribs on two large sheets of aluminum foil. In a bowl, combine the Louisiana spice mix or Texas rub, the paprika, onion powder, garlic powder, salt, and pepper. Coat the ribs with oil, then rub all over with the spice mix. Seal the foil tightly to create a pouch. Place on the grill over indirect heat and cook for 1 hour and 30 minutes.

In the cast iron pot, mix the beer, ketchup, molasses, brown sugar, and vinegar. Place on the grill over direct heat, and bring to a boil, then move to indirect heat and simmer for 2 hours until the sauce reduces by half.

Unwrap the ribs and brush them generously with the sauce. Grill on direct heat for 5–6 minutes on each side, basting regularly with the sauce.

Tip from BIG T

These are delicious with Coal-Roasted Sweet Potatoes (see page 240).

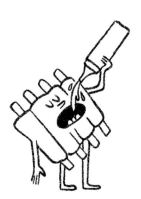

CARAMELIZED PORK BELLY
WITH CONFIT GARLIC PURÉE

Preparation Time: 20 minutes
Cooking Time: 5 hours
Cooking Method: Indirect heat

Equipment
Cast iron Dutch oven, aluminum foil

Type of BBQ
Gas, pellet, charcoal, kamado,
 smoker

Makes
4 servings

Ingredients
3 ⅓ pounds (1.5 kg) pork belly
¾ cup (180 ml) maple syrup, divided
5 medium yellow onions, peeled
 and quartered
20 garlic cloves, unpeeled, divided
1 bunch savory or thyme
1 bunch lemon thyme
¾ cup (180 ml) Maggi seasoning
4 cups (1 liter) olive oil
Balsamic vinegar
1 pound (500 g) Yukon Gold
 potatoes, peeled
⅓ cup (75 ml) crème fraîche
Kosher salt

Preheat the BBQ.

Using a sharp knife, score the fat of the pork belly in a crosshatch pattern.
Rub ½ cup (120 ml) of the maple syrup into the pork, making sure it flows
into the scores.

Scatter the onions, 10 of the garlic cloves, and the savory in the bottom
of the Dutch oven. Place the pork belly on top, fat side up, and top with the
lemon thyme. Pour in the Maggi seasoning and olive oil; it should partially
cover the pork, leaving the fat side uncovered. Cover the Dutch oven and
place on the grill over indirect heat. Cook for 5 hours, basting the pork
with its liquid every hour.

Place the remaining 10 garlic cloves on a large sheet of foil. Drizzle with
the remaining ¼ cup (60 ml) of maple syrup and a glug of balsamic
vinegar. Wrap up the packet and place over indirect heat for 20 minutes,
or until the garlic is softened.

While the garlic cooks, place the potatoes in a large pot of salted water.
Bring to a boil and cook until tender. Drain the potatoes and return them
to the pot. Add the crème fraîche and squeeze in the confit garlic pulp.
Mash everything using a potato masher. Season with salt to taste.

Unwrap the pork belly, slice it, and serve with the confit garlic
mashed potatoes.

PULLED PORK

Preparation Time: 10 minutes
Smoking Time: 8 hours
Rest Time: 30 minutes
Cooking Method: Indirect heat

Equipment
Injection syringe, butcher paper, spray bottle, smoking wood chips (cherry)

Type of BBQ
Gas, pellet, charcoal, kamado, smoker

Makes
6 servings

Ingredients
3 ⅓ pounds (1.5 kg) pork shoulder
½ cup (120 g) BBQ Dry Rub (see page 257) or another dry rub of your choice
1 ¼ cups (300 ml) apple juice
⅔ cup (160 ml) ginger ale
⅓ cup (80 ml) maple syrup
⅓ cup (80 ml) bourbon
⅓ cup (80 ml) BBQ sauce of your choice

Preheat the BBQ.

Trim any excess fat from the pork shoulder. Generously coat the pork with the dry rub to create a crust.

In a bowl, combine the apple juice, ginger ale, maple syrup, and bourbon. Pour half of the mixture into an injection syringe and the other half into a spray bottle. Inject the pork shoulder in ten different spots with the liquid mixture.

Set up the BBQ for indirect cooking by placing the charcoal on one side and a water pan on the other. Add wood chips to the charcoal for a delicate aroma and a nice coloration.

Smoke the pork shoulder for 8 hours, spraying it every 40 minutes with the apple juice mixture.

After smoking, check the internal temperature with a meat thermometer; it should reach 203°F (95°C). Wrap the pork shoulder in butcher paper and let it rest for 30 minutes.

Unwrap the pork and shred it using two forks. Mix the shredded pork with BBQ sauce and serve.

Tip from BIG T

Choose the pork rub of your choice; I particularly like the rubs from Angus & Oink and Firefly Barbecue.

Injecting the meat with the apple/ginger/maple/bourbon mixture adds a lot of flavor and helps tenderize it.

BOSTON BUTT STEAKS
WITH FRESH HERBS

Preparation Time: 10 minutes
Cooking Time: 20 minutes
Cooking Method: Direct + indirect heat

Equipment
Cast iron skillet, kitchen twine

Type of BBQ
Gas, pellet, charcoal, kamado, smoker

Makes
4 servings

Ingredients
1 bunch chives. minced
1 bunch parsley, minced
1 garlic clove, minced
4 Boston butt (pork) steaks
   (5–7 ounces/150–200 g each)
1 bunch thyme
4 tablespoons (50 g) unsalted
   butter
Olive oil
Pepper & Bourbon Smoky Joe
   Sauce (see page 250), for serving

Preheat the BBQ. In a bowl, stir together the chives, parsley, and garlic.

Sear the steaks over direct heat 4 minutes on each side. While they cook, preheat the cast iron skillet over high heat. Tie the bunch of thyme with kitchen twine. Melt the butter in the skillet, add the thyme and a drizzle of olive oil, then transfer the steaks to the skillet. Cook for 12 minutes over indirect heat, basting the steaks with the melted butter.

Remove the steaks from the skillet and roll the edges in the chopped herb mixture.

Serve with Pepper & Bourbon Smoky Joe Sauce.

MERGUEZ SAUSAGES

Preparation Time: 5 minutes
Cooking Time: 10 minutes
Cooking Method: Indirect heat

Equipment
Cast iron skillet or grill basket

Type of BBQ
Gas, pellet, charcoal, kamado,
  smoker, brazier

Makes
4 servings

Ingredients
2 Toulouse sausages
4 merguez sausages

❶ Preheat the BBQ. Clean and oil the grill.

Place an aluminum pan filled with 2 cups of water under the grill, next to the coals.

❷ Place the sausages on the grill above the water pan (take care not to pierce them). Close the BBQ lid and cook for 10 minutes without turning. The closed BBQ will function like a convection oven, ensuring the sausages cook evenly and remain juicy.

TIP FROM BIG T

Cooking the sausages over a water pan prevents flare-ups and keeps the sausages from burning.

THE LYNCHBURG

Preparation Time: 25 minutes
Resting Time: 2 hours
Cooking Time: 1 hour
Cooking Method: Indirect heat

Equipment
Injection syringe, cast iron Dutch
  oven

Type of BBQ
Gas, pellet, charcoal, kamado,
  brazier

Serves
2 people

Ingredients
Scant ½ cup (100 ml) bourbon
2 tablespoons smoked paprika
2 tablespoons BBQ Dry Rub
  (see page 257)
4 medium potatoes, quartered
Scant ½ cup (100 ml) white wine
2 Toulouse sausages
1 red onion, peeled and quartered
1 round Reblochon cheese
2 tablespoons fried onions,
  for garnish

In a blender, combine the bourbon, paprika, and dry rub.
Blend thoroughly and let the mixture sit for 2 hours.

Using the syringe, inject the bourbon mixture into the sausages
at both ends.

Preheat the BBQ.

In the Dutch oven, combine the potatoes, white wine, sausages,
and onion. Cut the Reblochon cheese in half and add it to the pot.
Cover with the lid.

Place the Dutch oven on the grill over indirect heat and cook for
45 minutes. Remove the lid and cook for another 15 minutes to
brown everything.

Serve sprinkled with fried onions.

Tip from BIG T

If you don't have a syringe, pour ¼ cup (50 ml) bourbon into
the bottom of the casserole before adding the other ingredients,
and combine the rest of the bourbon with the spice mixture and
sprinkle it over the potatoes and sausages.

BIG T'S
BEER CAN SAUSAGES

Preparation Time: 10 minutes
Cooking Time: 20 minutes
Cooking Method: Direct heat

Type of BBQ
Gas, pellet, charcoal, kamado, smoker

Serves
4 people

Ingredients
4 Toulouse sausages
4 (16-ounce) cans dark beer
2 onions, thinly sliced
4 sprigs rosemary
4 sprigs thyme
4 tablespoons BBQ Dry Rub
  (see page 257)
BBQ sauce of your choice,
  for serving

Preheat the BBQ.

Use a can opener to remove the entire top from the beer cans. Pour the beer into a bowl.

Place a sausage into each beer can. Add ¼ of the onions, 1 sprig rosemary, 1 sprig thyme, and 1 tablespoon dry rub to each can.

Place the beer cans on the grill over direct heat. Pour the beer from the bowl back into the cans, dividing it evenly, and close the BBQ lid. Bring to a boil, and cook for 20 minutes, flipping the sausages once halfway through. Add more beer or water if the liquid is evaporating too quickly.

Slice the sausages and enjoy with your choice of sauce.

Tip from BIG T

This recipe also works well with whisky- or rum-flavored beer and smoked sausages like Montbéliard.

SAUSAGE CASSEROLE
WITH RED WINE & ONIONS

Preparation Time: 20 minutes
Cooking Time: 1 hour 30 minutes
Cooking Method: Indirect heat

Equipment
Cast iron Dutch oven

Type of BBQ
Gas, pellet, charcoal, kamado,
  smoker, brazier

Makes
4 servings

Ingredients
4 Toulouse sausages
4 cups (1 liter) full-bodied red wine
4 red onions, quartered
4 garlic cloves, peeled
9 ounces (250 g) smoked bacon,
  cubed
4 sprigs thyme
2 star anise pods (optional)
Smashed Potatoes (see page 216),
  for serving

Preheat the BBQ.

Place the sausages in the Dutch oven. Add the red wine, onions, garlic, bacon, thyme, and star anise. Cover with the lid.

Place the Dutch oven on the grill over indirect heat, and close the BBQ lid. Cook for 1 hour and 30 minutes.

Serve the sausages with Smashed Potatoes.

Tip from BIG T

You can replace Toulouse sausages with smoked sausages like Montbéliard for a different flavor profile.

CROQUE MONSIEUR
WITH SMOKED HAM & REBLOCHON

Preparation Time: 20 minutes
Cooking Time: 20 minutes
Cooking Method: Indirect heat

Equipment
Griddle or grill plate, burger press
   or cast iron skillet, burger dome or
   aluminum foil

Type of BBQ
Gas, pellet, charcoal, kamado,
   smoker, brazier

Serves
4 people

Ingredients
3 tablespoons unsalted butter
4 slices country bread
4 red onions, sliced
1¼ cups (200 ml) maple syrup
1 pound (500 g) Reblochon cheese,
   sliced ½ inch (about 1 cm) thick
4 slices Gaspard's Smoked Ham
   with Maple Syrup (see page 146)
   or regular ham
1 bunch parsley, chopped
5 ⅓ ounces (150 g) grated Beaufort
   cheese (or Gruyère)
Grilled Little Gems (see page 218),
   for serving

Preheat the BBQ.

Place the griddle or grill plate on the grill over indirect heat. Add the butter, and when it melts, add the bread and toast on both sides until golden. Remove and set aside.

Place the onions on the grill plate, pour the maple syrup over them, and let caramelize, stirring occasionally.

On a work surface, layer 2–3 slices of Reblochon cheese on each slice of toasted bread, followed by a slice of ham, caramelized onions, and chopped parsley. Add another layer of ham, Reblochon, onions, and parsley, then top with a second slice of bread. Hold back a few onions for topping.

Transfer the sandwiches to the grill plate. Use the burger press or cast iron skillet to press down on the sandwiches while they cook, allowing the Reblochon to melt.

Sprinkle the top of the sandwiches with the grated Beaufort cheese and remaining caramelized onions, then cover with a burger dome or aluminum foil. Once the cheese is fully melted, remove from the grill.

Serve with Grilled Little Gems.

CHEESE-STUFFED
PUMPKIN

Preparation Time: 20 minutes
Cooking Time: 45 minutes
Cooking Method: Indirect heat

Equipment
2 cast iron skillets, skewers,
  aluminum foil

Type of BBQ
Gas, pellet, charcoal, kamado,
  smoker

Makes
2 servings

Ingredients
1 small sugar pumpkin or round
  winter squash
1 round Reblochon cheese
Scant ½ cup (100 ml) white wine
½ pound (250 g) fingerling potatoes
Kosher salt
1 cup (250 ml) maple syrup
4 ½ ounces (125 g) smoked bacon,
  diced
2 yellow onions, thinly sliced

Preheat the BBQ.

Cut off the top of the pumpkin and remove the seeds. Place the pumpkin in the center of one of the cast iron skillets, and nestle a foil ring around it to keep it stable during cooking. Place the Reblochon cheese inside the pumpkin. With a spoon, create a small crater in the cheese, and pour in the white wine. Replace the top of the pumpkin.

Place the skillet on the grill over indirect heat. Close the BBQ lid and cook for 45 minutes.

While pumpkin cooks, peel the potatoes and boil them in salted water for 20 minutes or until tender.

In the other skillet, combine the maple syrup, bacon, and onions. Place the skillet on the grill over indirect heat, close the lid, and cook until the bacon is crispy and the onions are caramelized.

When the pumpkin is cooked, pour the onion mixture into the pumpkin and stir to combine it with the melted cheese.

Skewer the potatoes and dip them into the melted Reblochon, as you would with a fondue.

GASPARD'S SMOKED HAM
WITH MAPLE SYRUP

Preparation Time: 20 minutes
Cooking Time: 3 hours 45 minutes
Smoking Time: 4 hours
Cooking Method: Indirect heat, hot smoking

Equipment
Large cast iron pot with a lid or Dutch oven, butcher paper, smoking wood chips (hickory or cherry)

Type of BBQ
Gas, pellet, charcoal, kamado, smoker

Serves
6 people

Ingredients
1 (7-pound/3 kg) pork leg, skin removed
2 ⅛ cups (500 ml) sweet apple cider
2 ⅛ cups (500 ml) chicken broth
⅔ cup (150 g) brown sugar
2 black long peppers, or 2 tablespoons whole black peppercorns (ideally Timut)
10 juniper berries
2 ¼ cups (550 ml) maple syrup

Place the pork leg in the cast iron pot and cover it with cold water. Add the cider, chicken broth, brown sugar, peppers or peppercorns, juniper berries, and chicken broth. Cover, bring to a boil, and then reduce the heat to a simmer and cook for 3 hours 45 minutes.

Remove the ham from the pot and discard the water. Place the ham on a large piece of butcher paper and brush it all over with the maple syrup. Tie the butcher paper securely: wrap it 3 times one way, and 2 times the other way.

Prepare the grill for smoking. Place the wrapped ham on the grill and smoke at 158°F (70°C) for 4 hours.

Slice the ham and serve.

Tip from BIG T

In the world of barbecue, there are moments when tradition and emotion intertwine, where professionalism blends with passion. Today, I'm honored to share a story that embodies both tradition and emotion: the story of smoked ham, a precious legacy I share with my son, Gaspard. Every slice of this ham tells a story that goes back generations, a story steeped in tradition, love, and dedication. It's an honor for me to pass this legacy on to Gaspard, my son, who carries on this tradition with the pride and passion of the greatest pitmasters.

LAMB
CHOPS

Preparation Time: 20 minutes
Marinating Time: At least 6 hours
Cooking Time: 15 minutes
Cooking Method: Direct + indirect heat

Equipment
Meat thermometer

Type of BBQ
Gas, pellet, charcoal, kamado, brazier

Makes
4 servings

Ingredients
¼ cup (60 ml) olive oil
4 garlic cloves, minced
Juice of 2 lemons
12 lamb chops, 1½–2 inches (4–5 cm) thick
1 tablespoon chopped thyme
1 tablespoon chopped rosemary
Coarse sea salt and freshly ground black pepper

In a bowl, combine the olive oil, garlic, and lemon juice. Place the lamb chops in a large resealable plastic bag, pour in the marinade, close the bag, and turn to coat the meat well. Refrigerate for at least 6 hours and preferably overnight. Remove the chops from the fridge 30 minutes before cooking to bring them to room temperature.

Preheat the BBQ. Clean and oil the grill.

Place the chops on the grill over direct heat. Cook 4–5 minutes on each side, then move to indirect heat and cook until the desired internal temperature is reached. Sprinkle with the thyme and rosemary and season with salt and pepper to taste.

TIP FROM BIG T

Do not salt the lamb chops until the end of cooking, as they already have an aromatic base from the marinade. Depending on your taste, you can swap out the thyme and rosemary for savory, mint, or other herbs of your choice.

LAMB SOUVLAKI SKEWERS
WITH GREEK YOGURT SAUCE

Preparation Time: 15 minutes
Marinating Time: At least 6 hours
Cooking Time: 9 minutes
Cooking Method: Direct + indirect heat

Type of BBQ
Gas, pellet, charcoal, kamado, smoker

Makes
4 servings

Ingredients
1 pound (500 g) lamb tenderloin
Marinade:
¾ cup (180 ml) olive oil
Juice of 1 lemon
1 tablespoon chopped fresh thyme, plus more for garnish
1 tablespoon chopped fresh oregano, plus more for garnish
Yogurt Sauce:
¾ cup (150 g) Greek yogurt
Juice of 1 lemon
2 tablespoons minced parsley
2 garlic cloves, minced
2 red onions, thinly sliced
1 cucumber, seeded and diced
2 tablespoons chopped fresh mint
Coarse sea salt and freshly ground black pepper
Extra-virgin olive oil, for serving

Slice the lamb lengthwise into 4 strips, each 6 inches (15 cm) long.

In a bowl, combine the olive oil, lemon juice, thyme, and oregano. Place the meat in a resealable plastic bag, pour in the marinade, close the bag, and turn to coat the meat well. Refrigerate for at least 6 hours.

In a large bowl, combine the Greek yogurt, lemon juice, parsley, garlic, onions, cucumber, and mint. Season with salt and pepper to taste and finish with a drizzle of olive oil.

Preheat the BBQ. Clean the grill.

Thread the lamb strips onto skewers. Grill over direct heat for 2 minutes on each side to sear, then cook for 5 more minutes over indirect heat. Drizzle the skewers with olive oil, sprinkle with thyme and oregano, and serve with the yogurt sauce.

PISTACHIO-CRUSTED
RACK OF LAMB

Preparation Time: 20 minutes
Cooking Time: 32 minutes
**Cooking Method: Direct +
indirect heat**

Equipment
Cast iron skillet, meat thermometer

Type of BBQ
Gas, pellet, charcoal, kamado,
smoker

Makes
4 servings

Ingredients
2 tablespoons (30 g) unsalted
butter
2 garlic cloves, minced
1½ ounces (40 g) chopped
pistachios
1 cup (50 g) breadcrumbs
2 tablespoons chopped parsley
1 rack of lamb with 8 ribs
2 tablespoons Dijon mustard
Olive oil
1 tablespoon chopped fresh
rosemary, for garnish
Coarse sea salt

Preheat the BBQ.

In a small saucepan, melt the butter and sauté the garlic until softened.
In a bowl, combine the garlic, pistachios, breadcrumbs, and parsley.

Place the rack of lamb on the grill over direct heat and sear for 1 minute
on each side. Remove to a work surface.

Brush the lamb with the mustard, then coat it evenly with the breadcrumb
mixture. Drizzle with olive oil.

Place the cast iron skillet on the grill over indirect heat, then add the rack
of lamb, fat side down. Cook for 30 minutes. Use the meat thermometer
to check the internal temperature; the lamb is perfectly cooked when it
reaches 131°F (55°C). Let the rack rest for a few minutes, then slice and
serve with a sprinkle of rosemary and coarse sea salt.

MILK-FED LAMB SHOULDER
WITH CONFIT GARLIC

Preparation Time: 20 minutes
Cooking Time: 7 hours
Cooking Method: Indirect heat

Equipment
Cast iron pot with a lid or Dutch
 oven, butcher paper, cast iron
 saucepan, aluminum foil

Type of BBQ
Gas, pellet, charcoal, kamado,
 smoker

Makes
4 servings

Ingredients
3 ⅓ pounds (1.5 kg) lamb shoulder
33 garlic cloves, unpeeled, divided
¾ cup (200 ml) maple syrup, divided
5 yellow onions, quartered
1 bunch savory
1 bunch lemon thyme
¼ cup (60 ml) Maggi seasoning
4 cups (1 l) olive oil
2 (8-ounce) cans (500 g) flageolet
 or cannellini beans, drained
2 cups (500 ml) heavy cream
1 ¼ cups (300 ml) white wine
Kosher salt and freshly ground
 black pepper

Preheat the BBQ.

Peel 3 of the garlic cloves and cut them in half lengthwise. Using a knife, make several incisions in the lamb shoulder and insert the garlic halves into the meat. Rub the lamb with ¼ cup (60 ml) of the maple syrup.

In the cast iron pot, combine the onions, 15 of the unpeeled garlic cloves, and the savory. Position the lamb shoulder on top, then add the lemon thyme. Pour the Maggi seasoning and olive oil into the pot, making sure it reaches halfway up the lamb shoulder without submerging the top. Cover the lamb with butcher paper and then place the lid on the pot.

Place the pot at the center of the grill over indirect heat and cook for 7 hours.

Prepare an aluminum foil packet with the remaining 15 unpeeled garlic cloves and the remaining ½ cup (120 ml) maple syrup. Place on the grill next to the pot and cook for 30 minutes.

Let the garlic cloves cool and then squeeze their pulp into the cast iron saucepan. Add the beans, cream, and wine. Season with salt and pepper to taste, and place on the grill over indirect heat. Cook for 30 minutes.

Serve the lamb shoulder with the flageolet beans and sauce.

RED WINE-BRAISED LAMB SHANK
WITH MASHED POTATOES

Preparation Time: 20 minutes
Cooking Time: 4 hours 30 minutes
Cooking Method: Indirect heat

Equipment
Cast iron pot with lid or Dutch oven, butcher paper

Type of BBQ
Gas, pellet, charcoal, kamado, smoker

Makes
4 servings

Ingredients
4 lamb shanks
5 medium yellow onions, sliced
5 ⅓ ounces (150 g) carrots, peeled and sliced
9 ounces (250 g) smoked bacon, cubed
3 cups (750 ml) red wine
⅓ cup (40 g) all-purpose flour
2 tablespoons maple syrup
1 bunch lemon thyme
4 garlic cloves, unpeeled
1 pound (500 g) Yukon Gold potatoes
Kosher salt
¾ cup (200 ml) heavy cream
7 tablespoons unsalted butter
2 tablespoons chopped parsley

Preheat the BBQ.

Place the lamb shanks, onions, carrots, and bacon in the cast iron pot. Pour in the red wine and add water until the liquid covers the shanks. Cover the shanks with butcher paper and then place the lid on the pot. Place on the grill over indirect heat and cook for 2 ½ hours.

Remove the shanks from the cooking liquid and set aside. Stir the flour and maple syrup into the liquid in the pot. Return the shanks to the pot, add the lemon thyme and garlic, cover, and cook for 2 more hours at 300°F (150°C), basting every 30 minutes.

Meanwhile, peel the potatoes and cook them in salted water until tender. Drain and return to the pot. Add the cream, butter, and parsley, and mash until smooth. Season with salt to taste.

Serve the lamb shanks over mashed potatoes, topped with the red wine sauce.

GRILLED CHICKEN BREASTS

Preparation Time: 5 minutes
Cooking Time: 15 minutes
Cooking Method: Direct + indirect heat

Equipment
Meat thermometer

Type of BBQ
Gas, pellet, charcoal, kamado, smoker, brazier

Makes
2–4 servings

Ingredients
2 boneless skinless chicken breasts
Olive oil
2 tablespoons chopped parsley
1 garlic clove, minced
2 tablespoons smoked paprika
Kosher salt

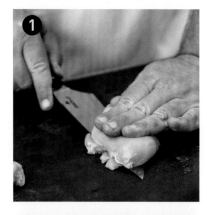

❶ Preheat the BBQ. Clean and oil the grill. Butterfly the chicken breasts (cut horizontally into the thickest part of each breast, then open it like a book).

❷ Brush the chicken with olive oil. Sprinkle chopped parsley, paprika, and minced garlic on the exposed chicken, then close the butterflied halves. Season the outside of the chicken breast with salt to taste.

❸ Place the chicken on the grill over direct heat and cook for 2 minutes on each side to sear the meat. Move to indirect heat and cook for about 5 minutes on each side. Check the internal temperature with the thermometer: it should reach 165°F (74°C). Slice the chicken breasts and serve.

TIP FROM BIG T

The key to perfectly cooked chicken is slow, low heat without ever placing the meat directly over the coals except to sear it.

CHICKEN SKEWERS

Preparation Time: 15 minutes
Marinating Time: 6 hours
Cooking Time: 15–20 minutes
Cooking Method: Direct + indirect heat

Equipment
Injection syringe (optional), skewers, meat thermometer

Type of BBQ
Gas, pellet, charcoal, kamado, brazier

Makes
4 servings

Ingredients
2 boneless skinless chicken breasts
4 lemons, quartered
Juice of 4 lemons
¾ cup (200 ml) fresh pineapple juice, optional
4 tablespoons sesame oil
1 tablespoon soy sauce
2 tablespoons chopped parsley
1 red onion, quartered
2 tablespoons Chicken Dry Rub (see page 256)
1 garlic clove, minced

❶ Cut the chicken into large cubes.

In a bowl, mix the lemon juice, pineapple juice (if using), sesame oil, soy sauce, and parsley. Inject the mixture into the chicken cubes using an injection syringe; otherwise, pour the marinade into a resealable bag.

Place the chicken cubes, onion, lemons, and dry rub into the bag with the marinade. Close the bag and turn to coat the meat well. Let marinate in the fridge for at least 6 hours.

❷ Preheat the BBQ. Clean and oil the grill.

Assemble 4 skewers by alternating pieces of chicken, onion, and lemon onto the skewers.

Place the skewers on the grill over direct heat and cook for 2 minutes on each side to give them a nice color. Move the skewers to indirect heat and cook for 10–15 minutes. Check the internal temperature with the thermometer; it should reach 165°F (74°C).

NEW ORLEANS-STYLE
CHICKEN WINGS

Preparation Time: 5 minutes
Cooking Time: 30 minutes
Cooking Method: Indirect heat

Equipment
Smoking wood chips (cherry), meat thermometer

Type of BBQ
Gas, pellet, charcoal, kamado, smoker

Makes
4 servings

Ingredients
2 ¼ pounds (1 kg) chicken wings
2 cups (500 ml) maple syrup
4 tablespoons BBQ Dry Rub
  (see page 257)
4 tablespoons Louisiana spice mix
2 tablespoons smoked chipotle powder
2 cups (500 ml) "Got You Babe" BBQ Sauce (see page 252)

Preheat the BBQ and prepare the smoker with cherrywood chips.

In a bowl, combine the chicken wings with maple syrup and toss to coat. In another bowl, combine the dry rub, Louisiana spice mix, and chipotle powder. Add the spices to the bowl with the chicken and toss to coat.

Place the chicken wings on the grill over indirect heat. Cook for 30 minutes, basting the wings with the BBQ sauce every 5 minutes and turning them every 10 minutes. Use the meat thermometer to check the internal temperature of the wings; it should reach 175°F (79°C).

Give the wings a final brush of BBQ sauce, let them rest for 5 minutes, and enjoy.

Tip from BIG T

Using BBQ sauce to finish the recipe is essential, and choosing a high-quality sauce is very important. If you're not making it homemade, I recommend the one from Maison Martin. You can also add spices before serving, or not, depending on your taste.

CHICKEN STUFFED
WITH CHORIZO & MASCARPONE

Preparation Time: 45 minutes
Cooking Time: 1 hour 45 minutes
Cooking Method: Indirect heat

Equipment
Food processor, meat thermometer

Type of BBQ
Gas, pellet, charcoal, kamado,
 smoker, brazier

Makes
4 servings

Ingredients
1 whole chicken (about 3 ⅓ pounds
 or 1.5 kg)
7 ounces (200 g) mascarpone
 cheese, divided
1 bunch chives, chopped, divided
4 garlic cloves, minced, divided
Juice of 2 lemons, divided
Olive oil
5 ⅓ ounces (150 g) mild Iberian
 chorizo, diced
1 slice country bread, cubed
Scant ½ cup (100 ml) white wine
2 onions, sliced

Preheat the BBQ.

In a bowl, mix half the mascarpone, half the chopped chives, half the garlic, half the lemon juice, and a drizzle of olive oil. Gently separate the skin from the chicken and spread this mixture under the skin, massaging it evenly.

In the bowl of the food processor, combine the chorizo, bread, wine, onions, and the remaining mascarpone, chives, garlic, and lemon juice. Process until a paste forms, and stuff the cavity of chicken with this mixture.

Place the stuffed chicken on the grill over indirect heat. Close the lid and cook for 1 hour 45 minutes. Check the internal temperature of the meat with the thermometer; it should reach 165°F (74°C). Serve hot.

Tip from BIG T

This method of preparing chicken, which involves adding a flavored fat between the skin and the meat, helps to infuse flavor and keep the chicken moist and tender. If you're more adventurous, you can slice some very thin rounds of chorizo (like truffle slices) and place them under the skin of the chicken after stuffing.

CHIMICHURRI-SPICED SPATCHCOCKED
SPRING CHICKEN

Preparation Time: 20 minutes
Marinating Time: 12 hours
Cooking Time: 1 hour 35 minutes
**Cooking Method: Direct +
indirect heat**

Equipment
Kitchen scissors, meat
  thermometer

Type of BBQ
Gas, pellet, charcoal, kamado,
  smoker, brazier

Makes
4 servings

Ingredients
⅓ cup (75 ml) olive oil
3 tablespoons red wine vinegar
2 scallions, finely chopped
3 tablespoons finely chopped
  cilantro
3 tablespoons finely chopped
  parsley
3 tablespoons finely chopped
  fresh oregano
½ jalapeño pepper, seeded
  and finely chopped
1 garlic clove, minced
½ teaspoon paprika
1 teaspoon ground coriander
2 poussins (young chickens)

Prepare the chimichurri sauce: In a medium bowl, combine the olive oil, vinegar, scallions, cilantro, parsley, oregano, jalapeño, garlic, paprika, and coriander.

Using kitchen scissors, cut out the backbone of each poussin and flatten them. Place the poussins in a large resealable bag with half of the chimichurri, ensuring they are well coated. Seal the bag and refrigerate for 12 hours. Keep the remaining chimichurri refrigerated.

Preheat the BBQ.

Place the poussins on the grill, bone side down, over direct heat. Cook 10 minutes. Flip the poussins so they are skin side down and cook for 50 minutes. Flip again and cook for another 35 minutes, basting regularly with the chimichurri.

Check the internal temperature in the thigh (without touching the bone); it should reach 165°F (74°C). Serve with the remaining chimichurri sauce.

CAJUN CHICKEN
THIGHS

Preparation Time: 25 minutes
Marinating Time: 12 hours
Soaking Time: At least 1 hour
Cooking Time: 1 hour 15 minutes
Cooking Method: Indirect heat

Equipment
Smoking wood chips (hickory)

Type of BBQ
Gas, pellet, charcoal, kamado,
  smoker, brazier

Makes
4 servings

Ingredients
4 free-range chicken thighs
¼ cup (50 ml) olive oil
3 tablespoons Cajun seasoning
3 tablespoons smoked paprika
2 scallions
3 tablespoons chopped cilantro
3 tablespoons chopped flat-leaf
  parsley
½ chili pepper
2 garlic cloves
1 teaspoon ground coriander
2 untreated limes

Brush the chicken thighs with olive oil.

In a mixing bowl, combine the spices, finely sliced scallions, chopped cilantro, chopped parsley, seeded and finely chopped chili pepper, peeled and pressed garlic, ground coriander, lime juice, and the squeezed lime pieces. Coat the chicken thighs thoroughly with this marinade. Place everything into a large resealable plastic bag, seal tightly, and refrigerate for at least 12 hours.

Fill a container with water and soak the smoking wood chips for at least 1 hour.

Preheat the BBQ.

Place the chicken thighs on the grill using indirect heat. After 30 minutes of cooking, place the soaked wood chips on the coals. Continue cooking for another 45 minutes.

Serve with Cajun rice (recipe on page 244).

Tip from BIG T

For a more intense flavor, marinate the chicken thighs in spices and lemon oil for several hours or overnight before grilling.

This recipe also works great with pork ribs.

CHICKEN BREASTS
STUFFED WITH VEGETABLES

Preparation Time: 25 minutes
Cooking Time: 20 minutes
Cooking Method: Direct +
indirect heat

Equipment
Kitchen twine

Type of BBQ
Gas, pellet, charcoal, kamado,
 smoker

Makes
4 servings

Ingredients
4 boneless skinless chicken breasts
Olive oil
3 tablespoons chopped chives
2 tablespoons chopped cilantro
3 tablespoons chopped parsley
2 garlic cloves, minced
1 teaspoon ground coriander
2 scallions, finely chopped
½ chile pepper, seeded and finely
 chopped
Kosher salt and freshly ground
 black pepper
2 red bell peppers
1 tablespoon brown sugar
1 onion, finely chopped
¼ cup (60 ml) white wine
2 tablespoons soy sauce
2 tablespoons maple syrup

Preheat the BBQ.

Butterfly the chicken breasts (cut horizontally into the thickest part
of each breast, then open it like a book).

In a bowl, mix 3 ½ tablespoons (50 ml) of the olive oil with the chives,
cilantro, parsley, garlic, coriander, scallions, and chile pepper. Season with
salt and pepper to taste.

Cut the bell peppers into very small cubes. Sauté them in a very hot pan
with a drizzle of olive oil. Add the brown sugar to caramelize them, then
add the onion. Deglaze with the white wine, stirring. Let the vegetables
cool, then add them to the olive oil-herb mixture.

Place ¼ of the vegetable mixture onto one exposed half of each breast,
then close the butterflied halves and secure them with kitchen twine.

In a small bowl, combine the soy sauce, maple syrup, and a scant ½ cup
(100 ml) olive oil.

Place the chicken breasts on the grill over direct heat and cook for
2 minutes on each side, then move to indirect heat and cook for
15 minutes, basting regularly with the maple syrup mixture.

Tip from BIG T

This is one of my favorite recipes: the aromatic base really elevates the flavor
of the chicken!

COOKING
GUIDE

DUCK BREAST
WITH MAPLE SYRUP

Preparation Time: 25 minutes
Cooking Time: 25 minutes
Cooking Method: Indirect heat

Equipment
Cast iron skillet, meat thermometer, aluminum foil

Type of BBQ
Gas, pellet, charcoal, kamado, smoker

Makes
4 servings

Ingredients
2 duck breasts (magrets)
Kosher salt
4 sprigs thyme
1 tablespoon unsalted butter
2 tablespoons maple syrup
1 teaspoon Espelette pepper

❶ Preheat the BBQ. Lightly salt the duck breasts by sprinkling a pinch of salt on the skin.

❷ Trim any excess fat from the sides of the duck breasts. Score the skin in a crosshatch pattern with a sharp knife, being careful not to cut into the meat.

❸ Insert the thyme sprigs into the cuts, 2 per breast.

❹ Place the cast iron skillet on the grill over indirect heat. Add the butter, maple syrup, and Espelette pepper. Place the duck breast skin-side down in the skillet and cook for 8 minutes, until the

skin is perfectly browned. Flip the duck breast, basting it with the rendered fat, and cook for another 8 minutes. Stop cooking when the internal temperature reaches 135°F (57°C). Cover the duck breast with aluminum foil and let it rest for 5 minutes before serving.

DUCK SKEWERS
WITH CHORIZO & BELL PEPPERS

Preparation Time: 25 minutes
Marinating Time: 12 hours
Cooking Time: 2 minutes
Cooking Method: Direct heat

Equipment
Skewers, meat thermometer

Type of BBQ
Gas, pellet, charcoal, kamado,
  smoker

Makes
4 servings

Ingredients
4 duck breasts
2 tablespoons olive oil
Juice and zest of 1 orange
2 tablespoons chopped fresh
  oregano
1 tablespoon coarse sea salt
2 piquillo peppers or bell peppers
1 mild or spicy Iberian chorizo

Trim excess fat from the duck breasts and cut the flesh into large cubes. In a bowl, combine the olive oil, orange juice and zest, oregano, and salt. Place the duck cubes in a resealable plastic bag, pour in the marinade, close the bag, and turn to coat the meat well. Refrigerate for 12 hours.

Preheat the BBQ.

Cut the peppers into large squares or keep the piquillos whole. Slice the chorizo into 1-inch (3-cm) pieces. Assemble 4 skewers by alternating pieces of duck, chorizo, and pepper onto the skewers.

Place the skewers on the grill over direct heat and cook for 1 minute on each side, or until desired doneness. Check the internal temperature of the duck with the meat thermometer; for medium-rare, it should reach 135°F (57°C).

Tip from BIG T

Replace the bell peppers with orange slices. Use rosemary stems as skewers—they'll add an incredible aroma!

FISH
AND
SEAFOOD

SALMON
IN PUFF PASTRY

 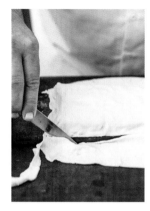  

Preparation Time: 15 minutes
Soaking Time: 24 hours
Cooking Time: 1 hour 15 minutes
Cooking Method: Indirect heat

Equipment
Cedar plank

Type of BBQ
Gas, pellet, charcoal, kamado,
 smoker

Makes
Scant ½ cup (100 ml) cognac
4 tablespoons orange zest
2 ¼ pounds (1 kg) wild salmon fillet,
 skin on, bones removed
2 tablespoons maple syrup
2 tablespoons kaffir lime oil
 or lemon-infused olive oil
9 ounces (250 g) puff pastry
1 large egg
2 large egg yolks
2 tablespoons chopped dill

Place the cedar plank in a large container. Pour in the cognac and orange zest, then add enough water (plus a weight) to fully submerge the plant. Let it soak for 24 hours.

After 24 hours, preheat the BBQ and remove the cedar plank from the water.

Place the salmon fillet on the plank. Trim any excess fat and score the skin in a crosshatch pattern. Mix the maple syrup with the kaffir lime oil and brush the mixture over the salmon.

Roll out the puff pastry and cover the salmon completely with it. Press the pastry onto the salmon, trim any excess, and score the pastry with a knife to create a decorative pattern. Prepare an egg wash by mixing the egg and egg yolks with 3 ½ tablespoons (50 ml) of water and brush it over the pastry. Sprinkle with chopped dill.

Place the plank on the grill over indirect heat and cook for 1 hour 15 minutes.

SALMON
WITH VEGETABLE CRUST

Preparation Time: 25 minutes
Soaking Time: 4 hours
Cooking Time: 1 hour 20 minutes
Cooking Method: Indirect heat

Equipment
Cedar plank, meat thermometer

Type of BBQ
Gas, pellet, charcoal, kamado,
   smoker

Makes
4 servings

Ingredients
Scant ½ cup (100 ml) white wine
1 red bell pepper, diced
1 green bell pepper, diced
1 medium yellow bell pepper, diced
2 red onions, diced
1 shallot, diced
1 small zucchini or yellow squash,
   diced
3 tablespoons finely chopped chives
3 tablespoons finely chopped
   parsley
1 scallion, finely chopped
1 wild salmon fillet
¼ cup (50 ml) kaffir lime oil
   or lemon-infused olive oil

Preheat the BBQ.

Place the cedar plank in a large container. Pour in the white wine and add 4 cups (1 l) water (plus a weight) to fully submerge the plank. Let it soak for 4 hours.

In a large bowl, combine the peppers, onions, shallot, zucchini, chives, parsley, and scallions.

Remove the cedar plank from the water and place the salmon fillet on top. Trim the fillet if necessary to fit it well on the plank.

Brush the salmon flesh with the kaffir lime oil. Cover the entire surface of the salmon with the vegetable mixture.

Place the plank on the grill over indirect heat and cook for 1 hour 20 minutes. Check the internal temperature of the salmon with the meat thermometer: for medium-rare, it should reach 115°F (45°C) at the center.

Tip from BIG T

The success of this recipe depends on the size of the vegetables and herbs—make sure they are very finely chopped!

TUNA
TATAKI

Preparation Time: 15 minutes
Marinating Time: 12 hours
Cooking Time: 12 minutes
Cooking Method: Direct heat

Type of BBQ
Gas, pellet, charcoal, kamado,
  smoker

Makes
2 servings

Ingredients
2 thick tuna steaks
  (about 7 ounces/200 g each)
1 tablespoon kaffir lime oil
  or lemon-infused olive oil
Juice and zest of 2 limes
1 scallion, chopped
3 tablespoons chopped chives
3 tablespoons soy sauce
3 tablespoons toasted sesame oil
Japanese BBQ Sauce (see recipe
  p. 251), for serving

Preheat the BBQ.

In a large resealable bag, combine the kaffir lime oil, lime juice and zest, scallions, chives, soy sauce, and sesame oil.

Place the tuna steaks on the grill over direct heat and sear for 1 minute on all sides, including the edges. Remove the steaks from the grill and transfer them to the bag with the marinade. Refrigerate for 12 hours.

Before serving, pat the tuna dry with paper towels and slice it into thin pieces.

Serve with the Japanese BBQ sauce.

SMOKED TROUT
STUFFED WITH HERBS

Preparation Time: 15 minutes
Soaking Time: 4 hours
Cooking Time: 1 hour 15 minutes
Cooking Method: Indirect heat

Equipment
Cedar plank, meat thermometer

Type of BBQ
Gas, pellet, charcoal, kamado,
  brazier

Makes
2 servings

Ingredients
½ cup (120 ml) bourbon
4 tablespoons Ginger & Lime Dry
  Rub (see page 257)
1 whole trout (about 1 ⅓ pounds
  or 600 g), cleaned
2 tablespoons kaffir lime oil
  or lemon-infused olive oil
1 scallion, chopped
1 red onion, chopped
3 tablespoons soy sauce
3 sprigs thyme
3 sprigs mint
2 lemons, sliced, divided

Preheat the BBQ.

Place the cedar plank in a large container. Pour in the bourbon and add 4 cups (1 l) water (plus a weight) to fully submerge the plank. Let it soak for 4 hours.

Season the cavity of the trout with the dry rub. In a bowl, mix the kaffir lime oil, scallions, onion, and soy sauce. Stuff the trout with this mixture, and tuck the thyme and mint sprigs in as well.

Remove the cedar plank from the water, line with half the lemon slices, then place the trout on top.

Place the plank on the grill over indirect heat and cook for 1 hour 15 minutes. Check the temperature; for a tender trout, it should reach 140°F (60°C) at the center. Let rest for a few minutes, then serve.

BIG MOE'S SARDINES
WITH CAJUN SAUCE

Preparation Time: 5 minutes
Cooking Time: 6 minutes
Cooking Method: Direct heat

Equipment
Food processor, cast iron skillet

Type of BBQ
Gas, pellet, charcoal, kamado,
  brazier

Makes
4 servings

Ingredients
1 bunch cilantro
1 bunch parsley
2 scallions
Juice of 2 limes, divided
1 tablespoon Maggi seasoning
3 tablespoons mayonnaise
1 tablespoon Dijon mustard
1 tablespoon harissa
1 tablespoon crème fraîche
1 pound (500 g) fresh sardines,
  heads removed
Fleur de sel

Preheat the BBQ.

In the bowl of the food processor, combine the cilantro, parsley, scallions, half the lime juice, and the Maggi seasoning. Process until smooth.

In a bowl, combine the mayonnaise, mustard, harissa, crème fraîche, and the blended herbs.

Place the sardines on the grill over direct heat (or on the preheated cast iron skillet over direct heat). Squeeze the remaining lime juice over the sardines and sprinkle with fleur de sel. Cook for 3 minutes on each side until nicely browned.

Serve the grilled sardines with the sauce.

GLAZED SMOKED SALMON
CUBES

Preparation Time: 25 minutes
Marinating Time: 12 hours
Drying Time: 30 minutes
Cooking Time: 2 hours
Cooking Method: Direct heat

Equipment
Cedar plank, cast iron skillet, food
    processor

Type of BBQ
Gas, pellet, charcoal, kamado,
    smoker

Makes
4 servings

Ingredients
2 tablespoons coarse salt
5 tablespoons brown sugar
1½ tablespoons garlic salt
1½ tablespoons paprika
2 tablespoons ground coriander
1 tablespoon freshly ground black
    pepper
½ cup (125 ml) maple syrup
4 salmon steaks
2 salmon fillets
1 pound (500 g) fingerling potatoes
Kosher salt
3 tablespoons unsalted butter
3 tablespoons chopped parsley
Pickled Red Onions (see page 258),
    for serving
Green Sauce
2 ounces (50 g) toasted pine nuts
3 garlic cloves, peeled
1 bunch parsley
Juice of 1 lemon
¾ cup (200 ml) olive oil

Preheat the BBQ.

In a bowl, combine the coarse salt, brown sugar, garlic salt, paprika, coriander, and black pepper.

In a dish, combine the maple syrup and ½ cup (120 ml) water. Add the salmon steaks and fillets and turn them to coat with the marinade. Cover the dish with plastic wrap and refrigerate for 12 hours.

Drain the salmon and pat it dry with paper towels. Let dry for 30 minutes.

Smoke at 320°F (160°C) on the grill for about 2 hours, basting the salmon with the marinade every hour. Let cool.

Cook the potatoes for 20 minutes in salted boiling water. Drain and dry the potatoes. Place the cast iron skillet on the grill over direct heat. Add the butter and parsley, then the potatoes, and sauté until golden.

Make the green sauce: in the bowl of the food processor, combine the pine nuts, garlic, parsley, lemon juice, and olive oil. Process until smooth, and season with salt to taste.

Cut the smoked salmon into cubes and serve with the potatoes, green sauce, and pickled onions.

FISH
CURRY

Preparation Time: 15 minutes
Cooking Time: 35 minutes
Cooking Method: Direct heat

Equipment
Cast iron pot or Dutch oven

Type of BBQ
Gas, pellet, charcoal, kamado,
  brazier

Makes
2 servings

Ingredients
Neutral oil
2 sea bass or haddock fillets,
  skinned and cut into 1.5-inch
  (3.75-cm) cubes
Unsalted butter
2 tablespoons grated fresh ginger
3 ½ ounces (100 g) asparagus,
  trimmed and cut in half
1 medium yellow onion, sliced
3 garlic cloves, minced
1 medium russet potato, peeled
  and diced
4 tablespoons Madras curry
  powder
1 (13.5-ounce/400 ml) can
  unsweetened coconut milk
1 red chile pepper
Leaves from 1 bunch cilantro,
  divided
2 scallions, sliced on the bias,
  for garnish

Preheat the BBQ.

Place the cast iron pot on the grill over direct heat and add a drizzle
of the neutral oil. Add the fish and cook for 1 minute on each side.
Remove the cubes and place them on paper towels to drain.

In the same pot, melt a knob of butter, then add the ginger, asparagus,
onion, garlic, and potato. Add the Madras curry powder, stir to combine,
and cook for 5 minutes.

Add the coconut milk, most of the cilantro leaves (reserve some
for garnish), and the chile pepper. Return the fish cubes to the pot.
Simmer for 25 minutes, stirring occasionally to reduce the sauce.

Sprinkle with scallions and the remaining cilantro, and serve.

ROASTED COD
WITH SAUCE VIERGE

Preparation Time: 25 minutes
Marinade Time: At least 3 hours
Cooking Time: 15 minutes
Cooking Method: Direct heat

Equipment
Cast iron skillet, meat thermometer

Type of BBQ
Gas, pellet, charcoal, kamado,
   brazier

Makes
2 servings

Ingredients
1 red onion, finely chopped
1 small red bell pepper, finely
   chopped
1 small green bell pepper,
   finely chopped
2 garlic cloves, minced
2 tablespoons sliced black olives
Juice of 1 lime
¾ cup (200 ml) olive oil
Kosher salt
16 ounces (450 g) cod fillet, skin on
1 tablespoon all-purpose flour
3 tablespoons unsalted butter
1 tablespoon grated lemon zest
3 sprigs thyme

Prepare the sauce vierge: In a large bowl, combine the onions, peppers, garlic, olives, lime juice, and olive oil. Add salt to taste, and let marinate for at least 3 hours.

Preheat the BBQ.

Coat the cod fillet with the flour.

Place the cast iron skillet on the grill over direct heat. Add the butter, thyme, lemon zest, and then the cod fillet, skin side down. Cook for 15 minutes, basting regularly with the butter. Check the internal temperature with the meat thermometer; it should reach 125°F (51°C) for medium.

Serve topped with the sauce vierge.

Tip from BIG T

You can replace the cod with another firm-fleshed fish that holds up well during cooking.

TUNA STEAK
WITH SAUCE VIERGE

Preparation Time: 15 minutes
Marinade Time: At least 3 hours
Cooking Time: 6 minutes
Cooking Method: Direct heat

Equipment
Cast iron skillet, meat thermometer

Type of BBQ
Gas, pellet, charcoal, kamado,
   brazier

Makes
2 servings

Ingredients
1 thick tuna steak (approximately
   400 g or 14 ounces)
1 tablespoon all-purpose flour
3 tablespoons unsalted butter
1 tablespoon grated lemon zest
3 sprigs thyme
Sauce Vierge (see page 192)

Preheat the BBQ.

Coat the tuna steak with the flour.

Place the cast iron skillet on the grill over direct heat. Add the butter, thyme, lemon zest, and then the tuna. Cook for 3 minutes on each side, basting regularly with the butter. Check the internal temperature with the meat thermometer; it should reach 125°F (51°C) for medium.

Serve topped with the sauce vierge.

COD SKEWERS
WITH PRESERVED LEMON

Preparation Time: 5 minutes
Marinade Time: 6 hours
Cooking Time: 5 minutes
**Cooking Method: Direct +
indirect heat**

Equipment
Skewers

Type of BBQ
Gas, pellet, charcoal, kamado,
  brazier

Makes
4 servings

Ingredients
2 ¼ pounds (1 kg) cod fillet, skin
  removed
4 preserved lemons, quartered
Juice of 1 lime
2 tablespoons curry powder
2 tablespoons sesame oil
2 tablespoons Maggi seasoning
¼ cup (50 ml) olive oil

Cut the cod into 1.5-inch (3.75-cm) cubes. Place cod and lemons into
a large resealable plastic bag. Add the lime juice, curry powder, sesame
oil, Maggi seasoning, and olive oil. Close the bag, and turn to coat the cod.
Let marinate for 6 hours in the refrigerator.

Preheat the BBQ. Clean and oil the grill.

Assemble 4 skewers, alternating pieces of fish and preserved lemon.

Place the skewers on the grill over direct heat and cook for 1 minute
on each side. Then move them to indirect heat, close the lid, and cook
for an additional 3 minutes.

GRILLED
OCTOPUS

Preparation Time: 15 minutes
Cooking Time: 1 hour 25 minutes
Cooking Method: Direct +
indirect heat

Equipment
Cast iron pot or Dutch oven, cast
  iron skillet

Type of BBQ
Gas, pellet, charcoal, kamado,
  smoker, brazier

Makes
4 servings

Ingredients
1 medium yellow onion, sliced
2 carrots, peeled and roughly
  chopped
3 bay leaves
2 Madagascar peppercorns
2 sprigs parsley plus 2 tablespoons
  chopped parsley
2 lemons
2 ½ pounds (1.2 kg) octopus
2 red onions, thinly sliced
Scant ½ cup (100 ml) white balsamic
  vinegar
6 ¾ ounces (200 g) fingerling
  potatoes
3 ½ tablespoons unsalted butter
2 tablespoons coarse salt
Brown sugar

Preheat the BBQ.

Place the cast iron pot over direct heat. Add 4 cups (1 l) water,
the onions, carrots, bay leaves, peppercorns, and the 2 sprigs of
parsley. Cut 1 of the lemons in half and add it to the pot. Bring to a boil.

Quickly dip the octopus into the boiling broth for 3 seconds, remove it,
wait 3 seconds, and dip it again for another 3 seconds. Repeat this one
more time. Then, submerge the octopus fully in the broth and move
the pot to indirect heat. Simmer for 1 hour and 15 minutes.

Once the octopus is cooked, cut the tentacles and let them cool.
Place them on the grill over direct heat and cook for 8 minutes.

In a medium bowl, combine the red onions and balsamic vinegar.
Set aside to marinate.

Cook the fingerling potatoes in a pot of salted boiling water for
20 minutes. Drain and cut them into cubes. Place the cast iron skillet
on the grill over direct heat and add the butter. When it melts,
add the potatoes, salt, and chopped parsley. Cook, stirring, until golden.

Cut the remaining lemon in half, brush it with brown sugar,
and place it cut-side down on the grill for 5 minutes.

Serve the octopus with the roasted potatoes, pickled onions,
and grilled lemon.

GIN-SMOKED
SCALLOPS

Preparation Time: 15 minutes
Marinade Time: 4 hours
Cooking Time: 15 minutes
Cooking Method: Indirect heat

Equipment
Smoking wood chips (apple),
   food processor

Type of BBQ
Gas, pellet, charcoal, kamado,
   smoker, brazier

Makes
4 servings

Ingredients
Scant ½ cup (100 ml) citrus-infused
   gin
1 red onion, finely chopped
2 tablespoons white balsamic
   vinegar
¼ cup (50 ml) yuzu juice
   (or lime juice)
10 scallops in their shells, cleaned
1 bunch cilantro
Olive oil
Kosher salt
Lemon zest, for garnish

In a medium bowl, combine the gin, onion, balsamic vinegar, and yuzu juice. Let marinate for 4 hours at room temperature.

Preheat the BBQ for hot smoking. Place the applewood chips on the coals. Place the scallops in their shells on the grill over indirect heat. Smoke for 15 minutes.

In the bowl of the food processor, combine the cilantro, a few drizzles of olive oil, and a pinch of salt. Blend until smooth and pourable, adding more olive oil if necessary.

Top each scallop with a spoonful of the gin marinade. Garnish with lemon zest and the cilantro sauce just before serving.

JFK
CLAM CHOWDER

Preparation: 25 minutes
Cooking Time: 35 minutes
Resting Time: 10 minutes
Cooking Method: Direct heat

Equipment
Cast iron saucepan, cast iron skillet

Type of BBQ
Gas, pellet, charcoal, kamado,
  smoker, brazier

Serves
2 people

Ingredients
2 round country bread loaves
  (about 14 ounces/400 g)
3 ½ tablespoons unsalted butter
1 small leek, white part only,
  chopped
1 onion, chopped
3 tablespoons all-purpose flour
1 ¾ cups (400 ml) fish stock
3 cups (750 ml) milk
1 medium potato, peeled and diced
Ground nutmeg
3 bay leaves
Kosher salt
⅔ cup (225 g) canned corn
5 ⅓ ounces (150 g) smoked bacon,
  cubed
20 small fresh clams, cleaned
Scant ½ cup (100 ml) white wine
2 tablespoons chopped chives

Preheat the BBQ.

Make 2 bread bowls: Cut off the tops of the loaves and set aside. Scoop out much of the inside of the bread and reserve for another use. Place the loaves (without the top) on the grill over indirect heat, and cook for 15 to 20 minutes to harden the crust. Set aside.

Place the cast iron saucepan on the grill over direct heat. Add the butter and, when it melts, add the leek and onion. Sauté for about 10 minutes, until they are very tender. Add the flour and stir for 1 minute. Pour in the fish stock and bring it to a boil.

Add the milk, potatoes, a pinch of nutmeg, bay leaves, and salt to taste. Simmer for 25 minutes, until the potatoes are tender. Remove from the heat.

Place the cast iron skillet over direct heat, and add the corn and bacon. Cook until browned. Transfer to paper towels to drain (do not clean the skillet). Stir the corn and bacon into the soup in the saucepan and let rest while you cook the clams.

Return the skillet to direct heat. Add the clams, deglaze with the white wine, and cook until the clams open.

Remove the clams from their shells (save a few in their shells for garnish) and stir the clam meat to the soup. Remove the bay leaves, and rewarm the soup if necessary. Ladle the soup into the hollowed bread loaves, arrange the reserved clam shells on top, and sprinkle with chopped chives.

CUBAN-STYLE
SHRIMP

Preparation Time: 15 minutes
Marinade Time: At least 6 hours
Cooking Time: 15 minutes
Cooking Method: Direct heat

Equipment
Food processor, injection syringe
(optional), cast iron skillet or
griddle/grill plate

Type of BBQ
Gas, pellet, charcoal, kamado,
smoker, brazier

Makes
4 servings

Ingredients
4 tablespoons chopped chives
1 red onion, chopped
3 scallions, chopped
4 garlic cloves, chopped
Juice of 2 limes
1 bunch parsley, chopped
2 cups (500 ml) olive oil
1 red chile pepper, stemmed and
seeded
3 tablespoons Ginger & Lime Dry
Rub (see page 257)
2 pounds (about 1 kg) wild-caught
jumbo shrimp or prawns, shells
and heads on
Scant ½ cup (100 ml) dark rum
1 lime, halved
Coarse sea salt
Cajun Rice (see page 244),
for serving

In the bowl of the food processor, combine the chives, onion, scallions, garlic, lime juice, parsley, olive oil, chile pepper, and dry rub. Process until smooth. Transfer the marinade into a syringe and inject it under the shell of each shrimp, then pour any remaining marinade into a resealable bag. (If you don't have an injection syringe, put all the marinade in the bag.) Place the shrimp in the bag and let marinate in the refrigerator for at least 6 hours.

Preheat the BBQ. Clean and oil the grill.

Place the shrimp on the grill over direct heat (or in the cast iron skillet, if the shrimp are on the smaller side). Cook, basting the shrimp regularly with the marinade. Depending on the size of the shrimp, this could take 2 minutes or more per side; look for the shrimp to turn a light pink color, become opaque throughout, and curl slightly.

Transfer the shrimp to the cast iron skillet. Pour the rum over them and flambé. Squeeze the lime halves over and sprinkle with salt. Serve with the Cajun rice or roasted potatoes.

SMOKY JOE'S
MUSSELS

Preparation Time: 20 minutes
Soaking Time: 5 hours
Heating Time: 2 hours
Cooking Time: 15 minutes
Cooking Method: Hot smoking

Equipment
8.8 ounces (250 g) smoking wood
  chips (maple), cast iron skillet,
  cast iron saucepan

Type of BBQ
Gas, pellet, charcoal, kamado,
  brazier

Makes
4 servings

Ingredients
Scant ½ cup (100 ml) bourbon
4 tablespoons chopped chives
1 red onion, finely chopped
3 scallions, finely chopped
4 garlic cloves, crushed
1 bunch parsley, chopped
1 bunch cilantro, chopped
1 red chile pepper, stemmed,
  seeded, and finely chopped
3 limes
2 ¼ pounds (1 kg) mussels, cleaned
⅔ cup (150 ml) heavy cream

Preheat the BBQ. Clean and oil the grill.

Place the smoking wood chips in a container, moisten the wood with water (it should be just damp), add the bourbon, and let it soak for at least 5 hours.

Add the soaked wood chips to a large sheet of aluminum foil, and fold it up to form a packet. Perforate the packet in a few places and move it to the grill. Close the lid and heat for 2 hours.

While the packet heats, in a large bowl, combine the chives, onion, scallions, lime juice, garlic, parsley, cilantro, and chile pepper. Cut the limes in half and squeeze the juice from 1 lime into the bowl.

Place the other 2 limes on the grill, cut-side down, and cook until charred.

Place the cast iron skillet on the grill next to the foil packet. Add the mussels to the skillet, close the BBQ lid, and cook until the mussels open. Squeeze the grilled limes over them and remove from the heat.

Place the cast iron saucepan on the grill and pour in the cream. Add the lime-herb mixture and cook for 5 minutes. Pour the mixture over the skillet with mussels and return the skillet to the grill. Cook for about 7 minutes, stirring until all the mussels are well-coated in the cream. Serve immediately.

BUBBA GUMP
SHRIMP

Preparation Time: 25 minutes
Marinade Time: 4 hours
Cooking Time: 5 minutes
**Cooking Method: Direct +
indirect heat**

Equipment
Food processor

Type of BBQ
Gas, pellet, charcoal, kamado,
  brazier

Makes
2 servings

Ingredients
Juice of 2 lemons
2 tablespoons curry powder
2 tablespoons Maggi seasoning
1 pound (about ½ kg) wild-caught
  jumbo shrimp or prawns, shells
  and heads on
2 tablespoons sesame oil
4 garlic cloves, peeled
¼ cup chopped parsley
¼ cup chopped cilantro
Juice of 2 limes

In a large resealable bag, combine the lemon juice, curry powder, Maggi seasoning, and the shrimp. Close the bag and turn to coat the shrimp. Marinate for 3 hours in the refrigerator, then 1 hour at room temperature.

Preheat the BBQ. Clean and oil the grill.

In the bowl of the food processor, combine the sesame oil, garlic, parsley, cilantro, and lime juice. Pulse until smooth.

Remove the shrimp from the marinade, slice them in half lengthwise, and brush them with the sesame oil mixture. Place them on the grill over direct heat and cook for 1 minute on each side.

Brush them again with the sesame oil mixture, move them to indirect heat, close the BBQ lid, and cook for an additional 3 minutes or until shrimp turn a light pink color, become opaque throughout, and curl slightly.

VEGETABLES

POTATOES

Boiling Method

In a large pot of cold water, add 1 tablespoon (10 g) of kosher salt per 4 cups (1 l) water. Add the potatoes. Cook for 20 to 25 minutes, depending on the size of the potatoes.

Always start cooking potatoes in cold water to ensure they maintain a firm texture.

Potatoes in Foil

Wrap potatoes in aluminum foil with a little kosher salt and 1 sprig thyme. Preheat the BBQ.

Grill Cooking

Place the foil-wrapped potatoes on the grill over direct heat, but not too close to the fire. Cook for 1 hour 15 minutes, turning them regularly for even cooking. Once the potatoes are cooked, open the foil, cut the potatoes in half, and top with 1 tablespoon of crème fraîche mixed with chopped chives and minced garlic.

Cooking in the Coals

Place the foil-wrapped potatoes directly in the coals. Cook for about 30 minutes, depending on the size of the potatoes. Then, place them on the grill and continue cooking for an additional 45 minutes. Open the foil and dress as desired.

Hasselback Potatoes

Cut the potatoes into thin slices, but not all the way through, so they stay in one piece. Between the slices, add a bit of olive oil or butter, herbs, or even cheese. Then, wrap the potatoes in aluminum foil and cook them as you would foil-wrapped potatoes.

Potato Skewers

Thinly slice the potatoes and alternate them with other vegetables on the skewers (zucchini, bell pepper, onion, etc.). It's important to make the potato slices thinner than the other vegetables, as they take longer to cook. (Or you can cut the potatoes into larger chunks and boil them until almost tender before skewering and grilling.) Cook over direct heat for 10 minutes.

Some Original Skewer Ideas:
· potato + chorizo + onion
· potato + smoked bacon + onion

Stuffed Potatoes

Cut boiled potatoes in half horizontally. Scoop out the flesh into a bowl with a spoon. Mix the potato flesh with ingredients of your choice (crème fraîche, bacon, onions, etc.). Stuff the potato halves with the mixture and sprinkle with grated cheese. Cook over indirect heat for 1 hour to 1 hour 15 minutes. Finish cooking under a burger dome or aluminum foil for 15 minutes.

Internal Temperature of Cooked Potatoes

· Small potatoes: 85–140°F (30–60°C)
· Large potatoes: 140–250°F (60–120°C)

JACKET
POTATOES

For 1 potato:
Kosher salt / ¼ cup (50 ml) white wine / 1 sprig thyme

Preheat the BBQ. Place the potato on a large sheet of aluminum foil. Sprinkle with kosher salt and top with the thyme. Drizzle with white wine and seal the aluminum foil to enclose the potato. Place the foil-wrapped potato on the grill, near the coals or directly in the coals, and cook for 30 minutes to 1 hour 15 minutes (depending on the size of the potato), turning it occasionally. Serve hot.

NORMANDY

1 cooked potato (see previous) / 7 tablespoons (100 g) crème fraîche / 3 garlic cloves, minced / 4 tablespoons chopped chives / 4 tablespoons chopped parsley / 3 ½ ounces (100 g) Beaufort (or Gruyère) cheese, grated

Remove the foil. Cut into the potato and open it to expose the flesh. Add crème fraîche, garlic, chives, and parsley. Sprinkle with the cheese. Place on the grill over indirect heat and cook for 15 minutes.

SAUSAGE
AND REBLOCHON

1 cooked potato (see previous) / 1 ½ tablespoons (20 g) unsalted butter / 3 ½ ounces (100 g) Reblochon cheese, sliced / 1 BBQ-smoked sausage, sliced / 4 tablespoons fried onions / 4 tablespoons finely chopped chives

Remove the foil. Cut into the potato and open it to expose the flesh. Add butter, Reblochon, sausage, fried onions, and chives. Place on the grill over indirect heat and cook for 15 minutes.

HOME SWEET HOME
BACON & REBLOCHON

1 cooked potato (see previous) / 7 tablespoons (100 g) crème fraîche / 1 onion, sliced / 4 slices grilled smoked bacon / 3 ½ ounces (100 g) Reblochon cheese, sliced

Remove the foil. Cut into the potato and open it to expose the flesh. Mix the crème fraîche and onion, then add it to the potato, followed by the bacon and Reblochon. Place on the grill over indirect heat and cook for 15 minutes.

FULL CHEESY

1 cooked potato (see previous) / 1 ½ tablespoons (20 g) unsalted butter / 1 slice ham / 1 tablespoon crème fraîche / 3 ½ ounces (100 g) Comté cheese, grated / 1 ¾ ounces (50 g) Cheddar cheese, grated

Remove the foil. Cut into the potato and open it to expose the flesh. Add butter, ham, crème fraîche, and the cheeses. Place on the grill over indirect heat and cook for 15 minutes.

SMASHED
POTATOES

Preparation Time: 10 minutes
Cooking Time: 35 minutes
Cooking Method: Direct heat

Equipment
Cast iron saucepan, meat
  thermometer, aluminum foil

Type of BBQ
Gas, pellet, charcoal, kamado,
  brazier

Makes
4 servings

Ingredients
5 large Samba or Yukon Gold
  potatoes
4 sprigs thyme
3 cups (700 ml) olive oil, divided
Coarse sea salt
½ cup plus 2 tablespoons (150 g)
  crème fraîche
1 bunch chives, chopped
3 scallions, finely chopped
2 garlic cloves, peeled and crushed
1 bunch rosemary

Preheat the BBQ.

Place 4 of the potatoes each on a sheet of aluminum foil with 1 sprig of thyme. Drizzle a scant ½ cup (100 ml) of olive oil over each potato and top each with a pinch of coarse salt. Seal the foil packets.

Place the packets on the grill over direct heat and cook for 30 minutes or until tender, turning them every 5 minutes.

Once the potatoes are cooked, remove them from the foil, cut in half, scoop out the flesh, and discard the skins. In a large bowl, combine the potato flesh with the crème fraîche, chives, and scallions.

Peel the 1 remaining potato and cut it into very thin matchsticks. Place the cast iron saucepan on the grill over direct heat, then pour in the remaining 1 ¼ cups (300 ml) of olive oil. Add the garlic and rosemary. Use the meat thermometer to measure the oil temperature. When it reaches 350°F (175)°C, add the potato matchsticks and fry until golden, about 5 minutes. Drain on paper towels.

Serve the mashed potatoes with the fried matchsticks on top.

GRILLED
LITTLE GEMS

Preparation Time: 10 minutes
Cooking Time: 5 minutes
Cooking Method: Direct heat

Equipment
Cast iron saucepan, meat
  thermometer

Type of BBQ
Gas, pellet, charcoal, kamado,
  brazier

Makes
4 servings

Ingredients
4 heads Little Gem lettuce
Scant ½ cup (100 ml) olive oil
2 garlic cloves, peeled
¼ bunch parsley
Juice of 1 lime
Scant ½ cup (100 ml) smoked
  balsamic vinegar
Kosher salt and freshly ground
  black pepper

Preheat the BBQ.

In the bowl of the food processor, combine the olive oil, garlic, parsley, lime juice, vinegar, and salt and pepper to taste. Process until smooth.

Cut the lettuces in half lengthwise, season with salt, and brush them with ¾ of the olive oil mixture. Place them on the grill over direct heat (or on the grill plate over direct heat). Grill for 5 minutes, until they are nicely charred and slightly translucent.

Brush the lettuce with the remaining olive oil mixture, and serve.

BRAISED FENNEL FLAMBÉED
WITH PASTIS

Preparation Time: 20 minutes
Cooking Time: 15–20 minutes
Cooking Method: Direct heat

Equipment
Cast iron skillet

Type of BBQ
Gas, pellet, charcoal, kamado,
 brazier

Makes
4 servings

Ingredients
1 pound (500 g) fennel bulbs, stalks
 and fronds trimmed
7 tablespoons unsalted butter
¼ cup olive oil
1 garlic clove, finely chopped
4 tablespoons chopped dill
Kosher salt and freshly ground
 black pepper
⅓ cup (80 ml) pastis
1 lime, halved

Preheat the BBQ.

Cut the fennel bulbs in half lengthwise.

Place the cast iron skillet on the grill over direct heat. Add the butter, olive oil, garlic, dill, and a pinch each of salt and pepper. Place the fennel halves in the skillet, cut side down, and baste with the melted butter using a spoon. Cook for 15–20 minutes, until the fennel is almost tender when pierced with a knife.

Pour the pastis over the fennel and flambé. Continue cooking until the fennel is tender.

Squeeze the lime halves over the fennel and serve warm.

ORANGE-GLAZED
GRILLED ENDIVES

Preparation Time: 15 minutes
Cooking Time: 30 minutes
Cooking Method: Direct heat

Equipment
2 cast iron skillets

Type of BBQ
Gas, pellet, charcoal, kamado,
  brazier, smoker

Makes
4 servings

Ingredients
3 ½ tablespoons (50 g) unsalted
  butter, divided
¼ cup (50 ml) maple syrup
Juice of 1 lime
¼ cup (50 ml) Grand Marnier
Juice of 1 orange
1 pound (500 g) endives
2 oranges, washed and sliced
  thickly
Kosher salt and freshly ground
  black pepper
Strips of orange zest, for garnish

Preheat the BBQ. Clean and oil the grill.

Place one cast iron skillet on the grill over direct heat.
Add 1 ½ tablespoons (20 g) of the butter, then add the maple
syrup and lime juice. Let it heat up. Add the Grand Marnier,
flambé, and then stir in the orange juice. Set aside.

Place the endives on the grill over direct heat and cook for
10 minutes, flipping them once.

Cut the endives in half lengthwise. Place the other cast iron skillet
on the grill over direct heat. Add the remaining 2 tablespoons
(30 g) butter. When it melts, place the endives in the skillet cut-side
down and cook for 15 minutes, flipping them once. Pour the Grand
Marnier-orange sauce over the endives and cook for
5 more minutes.

Let the endives rest a few minutes, then plate with the grilled
orange slices. Season with salt and pepper to taste, and garnish
with orange zest.

Tip from BIG T

Sprinkle some crushed walnuts and crumbled Roquefort cheese over
the endives before serving for an extra touch.

MAPLE SYRUP
CONFIT GARLIC

Preparation Time: 5 minutes
Cooking Time: 40 minutes
Cooking Method: Direct heat

Equipment
Cast iron skillet, aluminum foil

Type of BBQ
Gas, pellet, charcoal, kamado,
  smoker, brazier

Makes
4 servings

Ingredients
5 garlic heads
Scant ½ cup (100 ml) maple syrup
Scant ½ cup (100 ml) olive oil
2 tablespoons Butcher Blend spice
  mix (see page 256)

Preheat the BBQ.

Cut the garlic heads in half horizontally, and place them cut-side down in the cast iron skillet. Brush them with some of the maple syrup and olive oil, then pour the remaining syrup and oil into the skillet. Cover the skillet tightly with aluminum foil. Place it on the grill over direct heat and cook for 40 minutes, basting the garlic heads with syrup and oil after 20 minutes.

Press the garlic heads to extract the confit pulp.

Tip from BIG T

I use garlic confit a lot in dishes like tomato-based recipes, mashed potatoes, or to make a sauce vierge with crushed olives to accompany fish.

CARROTS
WITH CUMIN & LAVENDER HONEY

Preparation: 5 minutes
Cooking Time: 20 minutes
Cooking Method: Direct + indirect heat

Equipment
Cast iron pot

Type of BBQ
Gas, pellet, charcoal, kamado, brazier

Serves
3 people

Ingredients
1 bunch baby carrots, tops trimmed to ¼ inch (6 mm)
Scant ½ cup (100 ml) maple syrup
Scant ½ cup (100 ml) olive oil
Scant ½ cup (100 ml) white wine
1 bunch lemon thyme
3 ½ tablespoons (50 g) unsalted butter
2 tablespoons lavender honey
2 tablespoons ground cumin
Kosher salt and freshly ground black pepper

Preheat the BBQ. Clean and oil the grill.

Place the carrots on the grill over direct heat and cook for 2 minutes, then set aside.

Place the cast iron pot on the grill over direct heat. Add the maple syrup, olive oil, and white wine. Bring to a boil, then add the lemon thyme. Transfer the mixture to a large bowl and let it cool.

Return the same pot to direct heat and add the butter. When it melts, add the carrots, and baste them well with the melted butter. Add the maple syrup mixture, cover the pot, and move to indirect heat for 15 minutes, basting the carrots every 5 minutes.

Add the lavender honey and toss to coat the carrots until they are glossy. Sprinkle with the cumin and add salt and pepper to taste.

HONEY-GLAZED
BUTTERNUT SQUASH

Preparation Time: 5 minutes
Cooking Time: 30 minutes
Cooking Method: Indirect heat

Equipment
Large cast iron skillet, aluminum foil

Type of BBQ
Gas, pellet, charcoal, kamado,
  smoker, brazier

Serves
4 people

Ingredients
1 butternut squash, washed,
  top and bottom trimmed
3 ½ tablespoons (50 g) unsalted
  butter
1 bunch lemon thyme
Scant ½ cup (100 ml) verbena honey
¼ cup (50 ml) maple syrup
¾ cup (200 ml) white wine
Kosher salt and freshly
  ground pepper

Preheat the BBQ.

Cut the squash in half lengthwise. Scoop out and discard the seeds, then cut the flesh into 2-inch (5-cm) slices.

Place the cast iron skillet on the grill over indirect heat, and add the butter, thyme, honey, and maple syrup. Place the squash slices in the skillet and turn them to coat with the butter mixture. Add the white wine. Cover the skillet with aluminum foil and cook for 30 minutes, basting the squash regularly, until the liquid reduces and the squash is tender. Season with salt and pepper to taste and serve.

Tip from BIG T

Butternut squash is extraordinary. Its slightly sweet flavor pairs beautifully with the Roasted Cod with Sauce Vierge.

BRAISED
LEEKS

Preparation Time: 15 minutes
Cooking Time: 20 minutes
Cooking Method: Direct heat

Equipment
Cast iron pot

Type of BBQ
Gas, pellet, charcoal, kamado,
  brazier

Serves
4 people

Ingredients
4 leeks, trimmed to about 8 inches
  (20 cm) long so only white and
  light green parts remain
Olive oil
Sea salt and freshly ground pepper
2 garlic cloves, minced
3 sprigs thyme
2 tablespoons unsalted butter
⅔ cup (150 ml) white wine
⅓ cup (50 g) chopped hazelnuts
2 tablespoons chopped parsley

Preheat the BBQ.

Rinse and dry the leeks, then place them on the grill over direct heat.
Cook for 12 to 15 minutes, until outer leaves are charred and the cores
are tender. Remove the charred outer leaves and tops to keep only the
tender cores. Slice the cores thinly lengthwise.

Place the cast iron pot over direct medium heat. Add a drizzle of olive
oil, then add the leeks and season with salt and pepper to taste. Cook for
3 to 4 minutes, stirring frequently, until leeks are golden. Add the garlic,
thyme, and butter. When the butter melts, add the white wine and bring
to a boil. Cook until the wine is reduced slightly and coats the leeks.

Transfer the leeks to a serving dish, sprinkle with roasted hazelnuts
and chopped parsley, and drizzle with the cooking juices.

Tip from BIG T

Medium direct heat is best for this recipe; you can use the embers
from the end of another grilling session.

Alternatively, you can skip the hazelnut and parsley garnish, toss the
cooked leeks with a vinaigrette, and refrigerate to serve later.

GRILLED PIQUILLO PEPPER SALAD
WITH FETA

Preparation Time: 10 minutes
Cooking Time: 20 minutes
Marinade Time: 2 hours
Cooking Method: Direct heat

Equipment
Cast iron wok

Type of BBQ
Gas, pellet, charcoal, kamado,
   brazier

Makes
4 servings

Ingredients
1 ¼ cups (300 ml) olive oil
½ small red chile pepper, stemmed,
   seeded, and minced
6 garlic cloves, peeled, divided
2 ¼ pounds (1 kg) piquillo peppers or
   Padrón peppers
2 tablespoons brown sugar
¾ cup (200 ml) white wine
2 red onions, thinly sliced
4 tablespoons white balsamic
   vinegar
Kosher salt and freshly ground
   black pepper
5 ⅓ ounces (150 g) feta cheese
Chopped parsley, for garnish

Preheat the BBQ.

Place the wok on the grill over direct heat. Add the olive oil and heat until it begins to smoke.

Add the chile pepper and 4 of the garlic cloves. When the mixture starts to sizzle, add the piquillo peppers and brown sugar. Cook, stirring frequently, for 5 minutes, then deglaze with the white wine. Cook until wine is almost evaporated, another 5 minutes.

Once the piquillos are well-colored, remove them with their cooking liquid to a salad bowl, let them cool, and refrigerate.

Peel and chop the remaining 2 garlic cloves. Add them to the bowl with the piquillos, and add the onions and vinegar. Season with salt and pepper to taste. Let marinate for 2 hours.

On a large plate, arrange the chilled piquillos. Crumble the feta over them and drizzle with the onion-garlic vinaigrette. Sprinkle with chopped parsley.

EGGPLANT
TWO WAYS

Preparation Time: 25 minutes
Marinade Time: 2 hours
**Cooking Time: 45 minutes +
15 minutes**
**Cooking Method: Direct +
indirect heat**

Equipment
Cast iron skillet

Type of BBQ
Gas, pellet, charcoal, kamado,
  brazier

Makes
2 servings

Ingredients
2 tomatoes, cut in half
1 red onion, thinly sliced
2 garlic cloves, minced, divided
1 bunch chives, chopped, divided
1 bunch parsley, chopped, divided
Kosher salt and freshly ground
  black pepper
2 medium globe eggplants
Olive oil
3 ½ tablespoons (50 g) unsalted
  butter, melted
Leaves from 3 sprigs thyme
2 teaspoons dried oregano
3 ½ ounces (100 g) mozzarella
  cheese, diced

Dice one tomato half. In a large bowl, combine the diced tomato, onion, half the garlic, half the chives, and half the parsley. Season with salt and pepper to taste, cover the bowl with plastic wrap, and refrigerate for 2 hours.

Preheat the BBQ. Place the cast iron skillet on the grill over direct heat.

Cut the eggplants in half lengthwise. Score the exposed flesh in a cross-hatch pattern (do not cut all the way down to the skin). Brush the eggplant with olive oil and drizzle with the melted butter. Place them flesh-side down in the cast iron skillet and cook for 45 minutes, or until tender.

While the eggplant cooks, in a blender, combine the 3 remaining tomato halves with the thyme and oregano. Blend to a puree. Transfer to a bowl, add salt and pepper to taste, and then add a drizzle of olive oil, the remaining chopped garlic, and the remaining chives and parsley.

Remove the eggplant from the grill. Use a spatula to spread the tomato puree on two eggplant halves, then sprinkle with the mozzarella. Place the two halves on the grill over indirect heat, close the lid, and cook for 15 minutes.

Garnish the other two eggplant halves with the diced tomato mixture.

CONFIT
ONIONS

Preparation Time: 5 minutes
Cooking Time: 40 minutes
Cooking Method: Direct or indirect heat

Equipment
Cast iron skillet, aluminum foil

Type of BBQ
Gas, pellet, charcoal, kamado, brazier

Makes
4 servings

Ingredients
1 pound (500 g) red onions, peeled and halved
2 cups (500 ml) olive oil
4 tablespoons white balsamic vinegar

Preheat the BBQ.

In a large bowl, combine the onions, olive oil, and vinegar, and mix well to coat.

Option 1: Wrap the onions in aluminum foil and add 4 tablespoons of the oil/vinegar mixture. Seal the foil well, place it on the grill over direct heat or directly in the coals, and cook for 40 minutes, turning the packet every 5 minutes.

Option 2: Place the onions and the oil/vinegar mixture in the cast iron skillet with the marinade. Cover the skillet with a sheet of aluminum foil and place on the grill over indirect heat. Cook for 40 minutes.

SUMMER LOVE
SALAD

Preparation Time: 1 hour
Cooking Time: 30 minutes
Cooking Method: Direct heat

Equipment
Cast iron skillet

Type of BBQ
Gas, pellet, charcoal, kamado, brazier

Makes
4 servings

Ingredients
Olive oil
2 large shallots, peeled and halved
  lengthwise
4 garlic cloves, peeled
1 red onion, peeled and quartered
Kosher salt and freshly ground
  black pepper
4 piquillo peppers
3 ½ tablespoons (50 g) unsalted
  butter
Leaves from 2 heads Little Gem
  lettuce
4 ounces (115 g) cherry tomatoes
  on the vine
¼ cup (50 ml) white wine
1 large green cabbage leaf,
  for serving
2 tablespoons chopped parsley,
  for garnish

Preheat the BBQ.

Place the cast iron skillet on the grill over direct heat, add a drizzle of olive oil, and add the shallots, garlic, and onion. Season with salt and pepper to taste. Sauté until tender. Set aside on a plate.

In the same skillet, grill the piquillos with a drizzle of olive oil until well-colored. Set aside on the same plate as the shallots and onion.

Add the butter to the skillet, and when it melts, add the lettuce leaves and the vine of cherry tomatoes. Sauté until the vegetables color slightly. Increase the heat and deglaze with the white wine. Remove the skillet from the heat.

Place the cabbage leaf on a serving platter. Add all the cooked ingredients, sprinkle with chopped parsley, and serve.

Tip from BIG T

The secret to this salad is cooking the ingredients separately to create a perfect harmony of flavors. Feel free to add mozzarella balls or feta cubes, and top with your favorite vinaigrette.

COAL-ROASTED
SWEET POTATOES

Preparation Time: 10 minutes
Rest Time: 2 hours
Cooking Time: 30 minutes
Cooking Method: Direct heat

Equipment
Food processor, meat thermometer,
  aluminum foil

Type of BBQ
Gas, pellet, charcoal, kamado,
  smoker, brazier

Serves
2 people

Ingredients
5 tablespoons chopped chives
5 garlic cloves, chopped
Juice of 2 limes
Scant ½ cup (100 ml) olive oil,
  plus more for potatoes
Kosher salt
2 large sweet potatoes, unpeeled
¼ cup (50 ml) white wine
4 sprigs lemon thyme

In the bowl of the food processor, combine the chives, garlic, lime juice, olive oil, and salt to taste. Process until smooth. Transfer the sauce to a lidded jar and let it rest in the refrigerator for 2 hours.

Preheat the BBQ.

Rinse and dry the sweet potatoes. Coat them with olive oil. Place each potato on a sheet of aluminum foil. Add a pinch of salt, ⅛ cup of the white wine, and 2 sprigs lemon thyme. Seal the foil well.

Place the foil packets directly in the coals and cook for 30 minutes, turning them every 5 minutes. Check the internal temperature with the meat thermometer; it should reach 195°F (90°C).

Cut the sweet potatoes in half lengthwise and drizzle with 2 generous tablespoons of the sauce.

BRAISED RED ONION
SALAD

Preparation Time: 20 minutes
Cooking Time: 30 minutes
Cooking Method: Direct heat

Equipment
Cast iron skillet, aluminum foil

Type of BBQ
Gas, pellet, charcoal, kamado,
  brazier

Serves
4 people

Ingredients
1 pound (500 g) red onions
  (2–3 onions)
Olive oil
Kosher salt
4 sprigs lemon thyme
⅔ cup (150 ml) maple syrup
5 garlic cloves, minced
2 cups (500 ml) balsamic cream
  or balsamic vinegar
¾ cup (200 ml) red wine
5 ⅓ ounces (150 g) feta
5 tablespoons chopped chives
5 tablespoons chopped parsley
4 scallions, thinly sliced
Juice of 1 lime
Freshly ground black pepper

Preheat the BBQ.

Brush the whole, unpeeled onions with olive oil. Wrap each onion in aluminum foil with a pinch of salt and 2 sprigs of lemon thyme. Seal the foil tightly.

Place the foil packets in the coals and cook for 30 minutes, turning them every 5 minutes.

Once the onions are cooked, peel them, cut them into quarters, and set them aside.

Place the cast iron skillet over high direct heat. Add the maple syrup and bring to a boil. Add the onions and minced garlic, stirring well. Pour in the balsamic cream and stir to coat the onions. Deglaze with the red wine. Bring to a boil, then remove from the grill and let cool.

Once the onions reach room temperature, place them on a serving dish. Crumble feta over the onions and garnish with the chives and parsley. Drizzle with olive oil and the lime juice. Season with salt and pepper to taste.

CAJUN
RICE

Preparation Time: 15 minutes
Cooking Time: 30–35 minutes
Cooking Method: Direct + indirect Heat

Equipment
Aluminum pan, 10 x 6 x 2 inches
  (25 × 15 × 5 cm), aluminum foil

Type of BBQ
Gas, pellet, charcoal, kamado,
  smoker, brazier

Makes
4 servings

Ingredients
1 cup (200 g) jasmine rice
1½ cups (350 ml) chicken broth
2 tablespoons olive oil
5 tablespoons chopped chives
5 tablespoons chopped parsley
4 scallions, chopped
5 garlic cloves, minced
2 red onions, roughly chopped
5 tablespoons BBQ Dry Rub
  (see page 257)
1 teaspoon kosher salt

Preheat the BBQ.

In a large bowl, combine the rice, broth, olive oil, chives, parsley, scallions, garlic, onions, dry rub, and salt. Stir together, then transfer everything to the aluminum pan. Cover with aluminum foil and seal tightly. Poke a few holes in the foil.

Place the pan on the grill over direct heat. Close the lid and cook until it boils (about 20–25 minutes).

Move the pan to indirect heat, close the lid again, and cook for an additional 10 minutes until all the liquid is absorbed. Let stand for a few minutes, then fluff with a fork and serve.

MAC & CHEESE
WITH PULLED PORK

Preparation Time: 20 minutes
Cooking Time: 4 hours 15 minutes
Cooking Method: Direct + indirect heat

Equipment
Cast iron skillet, cast iron saucepan, aluminum foil

Type of BBQ
Gas, pellet, charcoal, kamado, brazier

Makes
2 servings

Ingredients
⅓ pound (150 g) pork tenderloin
Neutral oil
5 tablespoons BBQ Dry Rub (see page 257)
¾ cup (150 g) elbow macaroni
2 garlic cloves, minced
2 red onions, finely chopped
Scant ½ cup (100 ml) maple syrup
Scant ½ cup (100 ml) bourbon
½ cup (125 ml) heavy cream
1 cup (250 g) shredded cheddar
⅔ cup (150 g) shredded Beaufort cheese (or Gruyère)

Preheat the BBQ.

Place the pork tenderloin on a sheet of aluminum foil, brush it with oil, and coat it with the dry rub to create a crust. Wrap the foil tightly around the pork and place it on the grill over indirect heat. Cook for 4 hours. Let cool, then unwrap the foil and shred the pork with a fork.

Cook the macaroni according to package instructions, drain, and set aside.

Place the cast iron skillet on the grill over direct heat. Add the garlic, onions, and maple syrup. Cook, stirring, until the onions are caramelized. Add the bourbon and flambé. Clean out the skillet.

Place the cast iron saucepan on the grill over direct heat. Add the cream, then add the maple-onion mixture. Cook for 20 minutes, stirring occasionally. Add the cheeses and stir until melted.

Transfer the cooked macaroni to the skillet and pour the cheese sauce over it. Mix well. Top with the shredded pork.

Place the skillet on the grill over indirect heat. Cook for 15 minutes.

SAUCES, MARINADES, ETC.

CHEDDAR SAUCE
WITH CONFIT ONIONS

This sauce is a good match for meat, poultry, and tacos.

5 yellow onions, thinly sliced / Scant ½ cup (100 ml) maple syrup / ½ cup (125 ml) heavy cream / 1 beef bouillon cube / 1 tablespoon (15 ml) Maggi seasoning / Scant ½ cup (100 ml) bourbon / 5 ⅓ ounces (150 g) white cheddar cheese, grated

Preheat the BBQ. Place a cast iron skillet on the grill over direct heat and add the onions and maple syrup. Cook until slightly softened. Cover the skillet with aluminum foil, move to indirect heat, and let the onions caramelize for 20 minutes. Place a cast iron saucepan on the grill over direct heat. Add the cream, bouillon cube, and Maggi seasoning, and stir well. Add the bourbon and bring to a boil. Add the grated cheddar and caramelized onions. Stir well and move the saucepan to indirect heat for 30 minutes.

PEPPER & BOURBON
SMOKY JOE SAUCE

This sauce goes well with meat and poultry.

2 long peppers, or 2 tablespoons black peppercorns / ½ cup (125 ml) heavy cream / 2 beef bouillon cubes / 1 tablespoon Maggi seasoning / Scant ½ cup (100 ml) bourbon / Scant ½ cup (100 ml) maple syrup

Preheat the BBQ. Place a cast iron skillet on the grill over direct heat and toast the long peppers for a few moments. Let cool, then grind into a fine powder. Place a saucepan on the grill over direct heat and add the cream, bouillon cubes, and Maggi seasoning. Stir well, then stir in the bourbon and maple syrup and bring to a boil. Stir in the ground pepper and move the saucepan to indirect heat for 30 minutes.

GARLIC CONFIT
MAYO

Garlic Confit: 10 garlic cloves, unpeeled / Olive oil / ¼ cup (50 ml) maple syrup / 2 sprigs thyme / 1 tablespoon (15 ml) grated lemon zest / Kosher salt and freshly ground black pepper
Mayonnaise: 1 large egg yolk / Kosher salt and freshly ground black pepper / 1 tablespoon strong mustard / 1 tablespoon apple cider vinegar / Scant ½ cup (100 ml) neutral oil / 1 tablespoon herbs or spices of your choice

Make the garlic confit: Preheat the BBQ. Place the garlic cloves in a small aluminum pan, then add enough olive oil to cover. Add the maple syrup, thyme, lemon zest, and a pinch each of salt and pepper. Place the pan on the grill over direct heat for 20 minutes. Move the pan to indirect heat and cook for another 30 minutes. Remove the garlic cloves from the oil with a slotted spoon, squeeze out the garlic pulp, and mash it to a paste with a fork.
Make the mayonnaise: In a bowl, mix the egg yolk with a pinch each of salt and pepper and the mustard and vinegar. Whisking continuously, slowly drizzle in the oil until the mayonnaise thickens. Add herbs or spices as desired. Add the mashed garlic confit to the mayonnaise, stir to combine, and refrigerate for at least 2 hours before serving.

JAPANESE
BBQ SAUCE

This sauce, popular in Japan, is perfect for basting and as a marinade, especially for chicken.

½ cup smoked BBQ sauce of your choice / 1 tablespoon mirin / 1 tablespoon toasted sesame oil / 3 garlic cloves, pressed / 1 tablespoon grated ginger / 1 tablespoon red pepper flakes / 1 tablespoon white sesame seeds

In a bowl, combine the BBQ sauce, mirin, sesame oil, garlic, ginger, and crushed red pepper flakes. Refrigerate the mixture for 4 hours to allow the flavors to meld together. Before serving, sprinkle the sauce with white sesame seeds.

Tip from BIG T

All sauces can be prepared without a barbecue. High heat replaces direct cooking, and low heat replaces indirect cooking. Most sauce recipes make 4 servings (except for the ketchup recipe on this page, which serves 12).

Sterilizing Jars

While preparing the sauces, sterilize the jars by immersing them in boiling water for 15≈minutes. Once the jars are filled with sauce, place them back in a large pot of water and boil for 15 minutes.

MISS CHARLIE'S
KETCHUP

24 Roma tomatoes / 6 yellow onions, diced / 2 red bell peppers, stemmed, seeded, and diced / 2 cups (500 ml) white balsamic vinegar / 6 cups (1.25 kg) brown sugar / 2 tablespoons Butcher Blend spice mix (see page 256) / 2 tablespoons kosher salt / 2 tablespoons smoked paprika

Bring a large pot of water to a boil. With the tip of a knife, make a small X on the base of each tomato. Lower the tomatoes into the boiling water for 30 seconds and remove them with a slotted spoon. Let cool slightly, then peel. Preheat the BBQ. In a large cast iron pot, combine the tomatoes, onions, peppers, vinegar, brown sugar, spice mix, salt, and paprika. Place the pot on the grill over direct heat and bring the mixture to a boil, stirring frequently. Reduce the heat to medium and simmer uncovered for about 1 hour and 15 minutes, stirring occasionally to prevent sticking. Blend the sauce while still hot, then strain it through a sieve to remove any solids. Pour the hot ketchup into sterilized jars. Let them cool before sealing. The ketchup can be stored for up to 1 year if sterilized properly.

Unsterilized ketchup can be kept in the refrigerator for up to 3 weeks.

"GOT YOU BABE"
BBQ SAUCE

2 tablespoons smoked olive oil / 3 tablespoons molasses / 1 tablespoon apple cider vinegar / 1 tablespoon mustard seeds / 1 tablespoon Miss Charlie's Ketchup (see recipe above) / ¼ cup Worcestershire sauce / 3 tablespoons BBQ Dry Rub (see page 257) / 3 tablespoons smoked paprika / ¼ cup (50 ml) bourbon

Preheat the BBQ. In a large cast iron pot, combine all the ingredients. Place the pot on the grill over direct heat and bring the mixture to a boil, stirring frequently. Move the pot to indirect heat and let it simmer uncovered for 3 hours, stirring occasionally. Pour the sauce into a sterilized jar. Let cool before sealing. Properly sterilized, this sauce can be stored for up to 1 year.

Unsterilized sauce should be kept in the refrigerator and used within 3 weeks.

HERB AND VINEGAR
SAUCE

This sauce is ideal for French fries, fish and chips, or a fish burger.

1 tablespoon smoked olive oil / 1 tablespoon apple cider vinegar / 1 tablespoon chopped chives / 1 tablespoon chopped parsley / 2 garlic cloves, peeled / Kosher salt and freshly ground black pepper / ¼ cup homemade mayonnaise (see page 251) or storebought mayonnaise

In the bowl of a food processor, combine the olive oil, vinegar, chives, parsley, garlic, and a pinch each of salt and pepper. Process until smooth. Transfer the mixture to a bowl, then add the homemade mayonnaise and mix thoroughly. Refrigerate for at least 2 hours before serving.

CHIMICHURRI
SAUCE

To use this as a marinade rather than a sauce, add more olive oil.

2 garlic cloves, minced / 1 tablespoon finely chopped parsley / 1 tablespoon finely chopped cilantro / 1 small red chile pepper, stemmed, seeded, and minced / 1 tablespoon dried oregano / 1 tablespoon red wine vinegar / 2 tablespoons olive oil

In a medium bowl, combine the garlic, parsley, cilantro, chile pepper, and oregano. Add the red wine vinegar and olive oil, stirring well to combine.

The sauce can be stored in the refrigerator for up to 2 weeks or frozen in ice-cube trays for up to 3 months.

Note by BIG T

All flavored butters can be prepared without a barbecue. High heat replaces direct cooking, and low heat replaces indirect cooking. All butter recipes serve 4 people.

To Store Flavored Butter:

On a clean surface, lay out some plastic wrap. Use a spoon to shape the butter into an egg shape (quenelle), then place it on the plastic wrap. Roll it up tightly into an even log. Store in the refrigerator for up to 2 weeks or in the freezer for up to 3 months, and cut off pieces as needed.

PARSLEY & CONFIT GARLIC
BUTTER

This butter is ideal for pairing with beef and poultry.

Cloves from 2 heads garlic / Smoked olive oil / 1 tablespoon maple syrup / ¼ cup (50 ml) bourbon / 9 tablespoons (125 g) salted butter, at room temperature / 4 sprigs parsley, chopped

Preheat the BBQ. Place the garlic cloves in a small cast iron saucepan and pour in just enough olive oil to cover. Add the maple syrup and bourbon. Place the saucepan on the grill over indirect heat and cook uncovered for 2 hours, stirring occasionally. Once the garlic is soft and caramelized, remove the cloves from their skins and mash them into a paste using a fork. In a bowl, mix the mashed garlic and the butter until smooth. Stir in the chopped parsley.

THYME & LEMON CONFIT
BUTTER

This butter pairs beautifully with fish and lamb.

Zest of 2 lemons / 2 tablespoons smoked olive oil / 1 tablespoon maple syrup / 1 ½ tablespoons lemon-flavored gin / 2 sprigs lemon thyme, divided / 9 tablespoons (125 g) salted butter, at room temperature

Preheat the BBQ. In a small cast iron saucepan, combine the lemon zest, olive oil, maple syrup, gin, and 1 sprig of the lemon thyme. Place the saucepan on the grill over indirect heat and cook uncovered for 2 hours, stirring occasionally. Remove the thyme sprig and transfer the mixture to a bowl. Add the butter and mix until smooth. Strip the leaves from the second sprig of lemon thyme and mix them into the butter.

EL JEFE CHILE AND LIME
BUTTER

This butter is ideal for serving with fish, lamb, and chicken tacos (see recipe on page 62).

Zest and juice of 2 limes, divided / 2 tablespoons chile oil / 1 ½ tablespoons tequila / 4 tablespoons chili powder / 9 tablespoons (125 g) salted butter, at room temperature

Preheat the BBQ. In a small cast iron saucepan, combine the lime zest, chile oil, tequila, and chili powder. Place the saucepan on the grill over indirect heat and cook uncovered for 2 hours, stirring occasionally. Transfer the mixture to a bowl and mix in the butter until smooth. Stir the lime juice into the butter mixture.

SPANISH LOVER
BUTTER

This butter is perfect for serving with fish, lamb, shellfish, and chicken tacos (see recipe on page 62).

2 tablespoons chile oil / 1 tablespoon diced mild chorizo / 1 garlic clove, minced / 1 tablespoon chopped bell pepper / 9 tablespoons (125 g) salted butter, at room temperature / 2 tablespoons chopped sun-dried tomatoes / 2 scallions, chopped / Saffron threads

Preheat the BBQ. In a small cast iron saucepan, combine the chile oil, chorizo, garlic, and bell pepper. Place the saucepan on the grill over indirect heat and cook uncovered for 2 hours, stirring occasionally. Transfer the mixture to a food processor and blend to a coarse, sandy texture. Transfer to a bowl and mix in the butter until smooth. Stir the sun-dried tomatoes, chopped scallions, and a pinch of saffron into the butter.

CHICKEN
DRY RUB

Spice blend for poultry, pork, and vegetables

4 tablespoons sea salt / 1 tablespoon brown sugar /
1 tablespoon smoked paprika / 1 tablespoon dried onion /
1 tablespoon dried garlic / 1 tablespoon red pepper flakes /
1 tablespoon dried oregano / 1 tablespoon ground cumin /
1 tablespoon fenugreek / 1 tablespoon ground turmeric /
1 tablespoon ground black pepper

Mix all the ingredients in a jar and store at room
temperature, away from humidity.

This dry rub can be stored for up to 3 months.

BUTCHER
BLEND

Spice blend for meat, poultry, vegetables, and fish

4 tablespoons sea salt / 1 tablespoon red pepper flakes /
1 tablespoon ground black pepper / 1 tablespoon dried onion

Mix all the ingredients in a jar and store at room
temperature, away from humidity.

This blend can be stored for up to 3 months.

GINGER & LIME
DRY RUB

Spice blend for meat, poultry, vegetables, and fish

4 tablespoons sea salt / 1 tablespoon ground ginger /
1 tablespoon dried lime zest / 1 tablespoon dried onion /
1 tablespoon dried garlic / 1 tablespoon ground paprika /
1 tablespoon chili powder / 1 tablespoon dried parsley /
1 tablespoon ground black pepper

Mix all the ingredients in a jar and store at room
temperature, away from humidity.

This rub can be stored for up to 3 months.

BBQ
DRY RUB

All-purpose spice blend

4 tablespoons brown sugar / 4 tablespoons smoked paprika /
1 tablespoon dried onion / 1 tablespoon dried garlic /
1 tablespoon chili powder / 1 tablespoon dried oregano /
1 tablespoon ground cumin / 1 tablespoon ground coriander /
1 tablespoon ground turmeric / 1 tablespoon ground black pepper /
1 tablespoon dried marjoram / 1 tablespoon dried basil /
1 tablespoon dried tomato powder

Mix all the ingredients in a jar and store at room temperature,
away from humidity.

This rub can be stored for up to 3 months.

PICKLED
MANGO

For fish, club sandwiches, salads, poultry

Ingredients for 4 servings
½ cup (125 ml) white balsamic vinegar / ½ cup (125 ml) water / ⅓ cup (75 ml) maple syrup / 4 green mangoes / 4 black peppercorns

Preheat the BBQ. In a cast iron saucepan, combine the vinegar, water, and maple syrup, then place on the grill over direct heat and bring to a boil. Slice the mangoes into thin strips using a vegetable peeler and place them in a jar. Add the peppercorns and cover with the hot liquid. Let the mixture rest in the refrigerator for 2 days before serving.

The pickles can be stored in the refrigerator for up to 3 months.

PICKLED
RED ONIONS

For meat, poultry, vegetables, fish, plain rice

Ingredients for 4 servings:
½ cup (125 ml) white balsamic vinegar / ½ cup (125 ml) water / ⅓ cup (75 ml) maple syrup / 3 red onions, thinly sliced / 4 black peppercorns / 1 small bird's eye chile pepper, stemmed, seeded, and minced / 1 tablespoon Maggi seasoning

Preheat the BBQ. In a cast iron saucepan, combine the vinegar, water, and maple syrup, then place on the grill over direct heat and bring to a boil. Place the red onions in a large jar. Add the peppercorns, chile pepper, and Maggi seasoning. Cover with the hot liquid. Let the mixture rest in the refrigerator for 2 days before serving.

The pickles can be stored in the refrigerator for up to 3 months.

JAPANESE
PICKLED LEEK

For meat, poultry, vegetables, fish, plain rice, ramen

Ingredients for 4 servings:
2 leeks, white and light green parts / 1 tablespoon kosher salt / 1 red chile pepper, stemmed, seeded, and minced / 2 scallions, finely chopped / ½ cup (125 ml) sesame oil / 1 tablespoon Maggi seasoning

Slice the leeks thinly and let them soak in a bowl of water. Agitate with your hands to clean them. Strain the leeks and transfer them to another bowl. Add the salt and massage it into the leeks to break down the fibers. Transfer the leeks to a jar. Add the chile pepper and scallions. Pour in the sesame oil and Maggi seasoning. Let the mixture rest in the refrigerator for 2 days before serving.

The pickles can be stored in the refrigerator for up to 3 months.

PICKLED
CABBAGE

For meat, poultry, vegetables, fish, salads

Ingredients for 4 servings:
½ cup (125 ml) apple cider vinegar / 1 cup (225 ml) water / ½ cup (75 g) brown sugar / 5 ⅓ ounces (150 g) green cabbage, thinly sliced / 4 coriander seeds

Preheat the BBQ. In a cast iron saucepan, combine the vinegar, water, and sugar, then bring to a boil. Place the cabbage in a jar. Add the coriander seeds and cover with the hot liquid. Let the mixture rest in the refrigerator for 2 days before serving.

The pickles can be stored in the refrigerator for up to 3 months.

DESSERTS

RASPBERRY COMPOTE
WITH RED WINE

Preparation: 5 minutes
Cooking: 3 hours
Type of Cooking: Direct + indirect

Equipment
Cast iron pot

Type of BBQ
Gas, pellet, charcoal, kamado,
  smoker, brazier

Makes
4 servings

Ingredients
3 cups (750 ml) light red wine
¾ cup (100 g) brown sugar
2 vanilla pods, split lengthwise
10 ounces (300 g) raspberries
A handful of mint leaves

Preheat the BBQ.

Place the cast iron pot on the grill over direct heat. Add the red wine and sugar. Scrape the vanilla seeds into the pot with the tip of a paring knife and drop in the pods. Mix well and bring to a boil.

Add the raspberries and move the pot to indirect heat. Cook for 3 hours, until the wine has reduced by half and just covers the raspberries.

Remove from heat, remove the vanilla pods, add the mint leaves, and let cool.

Serve with vanilla ice cream or Greek yogurt.

RUM-FLAMBÉED ROASTED PINEAPPLE,
TWO WAYS

Preparation: 15 minutes
Cooking: 30 minutes
Type of Cooking: Direct

Equipment
Griddle or grill plate

Type of BBQ
Gas, pellet, charcoal, kamado,
 brazier

Makes
2 servings

Ingredients
1 ripe pineapple
1 lime, halved
1 ½ cups (200 g) brown sugar,
 divided
2 cups (500 ml) maple syrup
1 cup (225 ml) rum

Preheat the BBQ. Place the grill plate or griddle on the grill over direct heat.

Cut the pineapple in half lengthwise. Squeeze the lime juice over the flesh.

Sprinkle ½ the brown sugar over the pineapple to form a crust. Place the pineapple, sugar side-down, on the grill plate or griddle. Let cook for 15 minutes, until caramelized.

Pour the maple syrup onto the grill plate or griddle and continue to caramelize the pineapple. Press down on the pineapples to adhere the sugar. Pour the rum and flambé. Once the rum evaporates, turn the pineapples and sprinkle with brown sugar again. Cook for another 10 minutes. Let cool.

Cut the pineapples into cubes. Serve as is or with pineapple sorbet.

POACHED
PEARS

Preparation: 20 minutes
Cooking: 1 hour 20 minutes–
1 hour 30 minutes
Type of Cooking: Direct +
indirect

Equipment
Cast iron pot

Type of BBQ
Gas, pellet, charcoal, kamado,
  smoker, brazier

Makes
7 servings

Ingredients
3 cups (750 ml) red wine
1½ cups (200 g) brown sugar
2 tablespoons lavender honey
1 tablespoon orange zest
2 vanilla pods, split lengthwise
2 sprigs lemon verbena
7 Williams or Bartlett pears, peeled,
  stem left intact

Preheat the BBQ.

Prepare the syrup: In the cast iron pot, combine the red wine, sugar, honey, and orange zest. Place on the grill over direct heat and bring to a boil, then scrape the vanilla seeds into the pot with the tip of a paring knife and drop in the pods. Add the lemon verbena. Move the pot to indirect heat.

Add the pears to the syrup and cook for 1 hour 20 minutes to 1 hour 30 minutes, until tender.

Remove the pears and reduce the syrup for about 50 minutes until thickened. Drizzle the pears with the syrup and let cool before serving.

FRENCH TOAST
WITH FLAMBÉED BANANA
& CHOCOLATE

Preparation: 15 minutes
Cooking: 10 minutes
Type of Cooking: Direct

Equipment
2 cast iron skillets

Type of BBQ
Gas, pellet, charcoal, kamado,
  brazier

Makes
4 servings

Ingredients
4 large eggs
1 ⅔ cups (400 ml) heavy cream
2 vanilla pods, split lengthwise
4 thick slices brioche
4 tablespoons unsalted butter,
  divided
2 tablespoons brown sugar
4 ripe bananas
3 ½ tablespoons (50 ml) dark rum
  (optional)
2 tablespoons orange zest
7 ounces (200 g) dark chocolate,
  chopped

Preheat the BBQ.

In a bowl, whisk together the eggs and cream. Scrape the vanilla seeds into the egg-cream mixture with the tip of a paring knife and drop in the pods.

Place one cast iron skillet on the grill over direct heat. Add the butter. When it melts, dip the brioche slices into the egg-cream-vanilla mixture. Place them in the hot pan and brown for 5 minutes on each side. Serve each slice on a plate.

In the other cast iron skillet, add the remaining 2 tablespoons butter. Sprinkle in the brown sugar, heat the remaining butter and 2 tablespoons of brown sugar. Peel the bananas and add to the skillet, turning occasionally to help them caramelize. Add the rum, if using, and flambé. Stir in the orange zest. Remove the bananas. Add the chocolate to the skillet and stir until it melts.

Place each piece of brioche on a plate, and top with a banana. Drizzle with the melted chocolate sauce.

PAPPY BOYINGTON'S
BRAISED APPLES

Preparation: 15 minutes
Cooking: 50 minutes
Type of Cooking: Direct + indirect

Equipment
Aluminum foil

Type of BBQ
Pellet, charcoal, kamado, smoker, brazier

Makes
4 servings

Ingredients
4 tablespoons brown sugar
4 tablespoons maple syrup
Scant ½ cup (100 ml) Calvados
2 vanilla pods, split lengthwise
4 Golden Delicious apples
2 tablespoons unsalted butter, divided
4 cinnamon sticks

Preheat the BBQ.

In a bowl, combine the brown sugar, maple syrup, and Calvados. Scrape in the vanilla seeds with the tip of a paring knife.

Scoop ⅔ of the core out of each apple (do not cut all the way through). Place ½ tablespoon butter in the core of each apple, pour ¼ of the liquid mixture into each core, and place a cinnamon stick in the center of each apple.

Place the apples together on a large sheet of aluminum foil. Fold the foil over the apples to create a pouch. Create a ring of embers on the barbecue and place the apple pouch in the center. Cook for 10 minutes, rotating them after 5 minutes. Move the pouch to the grill over indirect heat and cook for 40 minutes.

Test for doneness by inserting a knife into one of the apples; the blade should slide in easily.

Let apples cool slightly and serve warm.

ROASTED MANGO
WITH MAPLE SYRUP

Preparation: 15 minutes
Cooking: 8 minutes
Cooking Method: Indirect

Equipment
Griddle or grill plate

Type of BBQ
Gas, pellet, charcoal, kamado,
  or brazier

Makes
4 servings

Ingredients
2 mangoes
Leaves from 2 sprigs lemon thyme
3 tablespoons maple syrup
3 ½ tablespoons (50 ml) bourbon
3 tablespoons thyme honey
Juice of 1 lime
3 tablespoons unsalted butter
Mango sorbet, for serving

Preheat the BBQ.

Cut the mangoes in half lengthwise and remove the pits. Score the flesh of the mangoes in a crosshatch pattern with a knife. Sprinkle the lemon thyme leaves into the cuts.

In a bowl, mix together the maple syrup, bourbon, honey, and lime juice.

Place the grill plate on the grill over indirect heat. Add the butter. When it melts, place the mango halves flesh-side down on the plate and cook them for 8 minutes, basting with the maple syrup-bourbon-honey mixture every 2 minutes.

Serve with 2 scoops of mango sorbet per person.

GRANDMA LÉA'S APRICOT
CASSEROLE

Preparation: 15 minutes
Marinating: 12 hours
Cooking: 1 hour 35 minutes
Cooking Method: Indirect

Equipment
Large cast iron pot, food processor,
  4 glass jars (12 ounces/330 ml
  each), aluminum foil

Type of BBQ
Gas, pellet, charcoal, kamado

Makes
4 servings

Ingredients
10 apricots
3 ½ tablespoons (50 ml) gin
2 tablespoons grated orange zest
4 tablespoons maple syrup
2 tablespoons verbena or lavender
  honey, divided
2 tablespoons brown sugar
Juice of 2 limes
2 vanilla pods, split lengthwise
4 shortbread cookies
2 tablespoons almond flour
4 large egg yolks
2 cups (500 ml) heavy cream

Preheat the BBQ.

Pit the apricots and place them in a bowl. Add the gin and orange zest.
Let marinate for 12 hours in the refrigerator.

Remove the apricots from the gin marinade and set aside. In the large
cast iron pot, combine the gin marinade (without the apricots), the maple
syrup, 1 tablespoon of the honey, the brown sugar and lime juice. Scrape
the vanilla seeds into the pot with the tip of a paring knife and add the
pods. Place the pot over indirect heat and cook for 15 minutes, stirring
with a whisk. Add the apricots and cook for 1 hour without stirring.

In the food processor, blend the shortbread cookies and almond flour
together until homogeneous.

In a bowl, combine the cream, egg yolks, and the remaining 1 tablespoon
of honey. Add the almond-shortbread mixture and stir well.

Distribute the apricots evenly between the jars, then pour the cream-
almond mixture over them. Cover the jars with aluminum foil and place
them on the grill over indirect heat. Cook for 20 minutes.

Let the jars cool in the refrigerator before serving.

BERRY
CRUMBLE

Preparation: 15 minutes
Cooking: 20 minutes
Type of cooking: Indirect

Equipment
Cast iron saucepan, cast iron skillet

Type of BBQ
Gas, pellet, charcoal, kamado

Makes
4 servings

Ingredients
Fruit Filling
5 tablespoons lavender honey
3 ½ tablespoons (50 ml) maple
   whisky (or 1 ¾ tablespoons
   (25 ml) plain whisky mixed with
   1 ¾ tablespoons (25 ml) maple
   syrup, macerated for 24 hours)
¼ cup (50 g) quartered strawberries
¼ cup (50 g) raspberries
¼ cup (50 g) blueberries
1 banana, peeled and sliced
1 clementine or mandarin,
   quartered
1 kiwi, peeled and sliced
Crumble Dough
¾ cup (100 g) all-purpose flour
½ cup (100 g) brown sugar
½ cup (100 g) almond flour
7 tablespoons softened unsalted
   butter, at room temperature
1 large egg yolk

Preheat the BBQ.

In the cast iron saucepan, combine the honey and whiskey. Place on the grill over direct heat and cook, stirring, until the honey melts. Set aside and let cool.

Make the crumble dough: In a bowl, combine the flour, sugar, almond flour, and butter. Work in the butter with your fingers until you get a crumbly dough.

Spread the crumble dough in the bottom of the cast iron skillet. Brush with the egg yolk, and place the skillet on the grill over indirect heat. Cook for 20 minutes, until the dough is golden brown. Let cool.

Arrange all the fruit on the crumble, alternating colors. Brush with the honey-whiskey syrup.

LIST OF RECIPES

FISH AND SEAFOOD

VEGETABLES

SAUCES, MARINADES, ETC.

DESSERTS

INDEX

THANK YOU

A heartfelt thank you to my cherished partners, suppliers, and those who believed in my vision and joined me on this journey with such enthusiasm and trust. Their names resonate as living symbols of commitment and invaluable support: Laurent from Brasero Industrie Concept, representing the excellence of French braseros; Aurélien from Yakiniku & Vulcanus; Alain from Big Green Egg; Arthur from Traeger; James from Kamado Joe; Patrice from Silex; Brian from Custom Woodwork; Marc and Guy from Slush, loyal companions since the beginning of this adventure; Alexis and Carole from BMW Moto; Manu from Atelier 1515, and my dear Loulou, who has been a lifelong bond; Julie from Woodmata; Élise and Jean-Xavier from Table Pro; and the dynamic duo from Massimo Cucine, among so many others.

To Carlos from La Sirène Fishery; Christian and René from Sup Viandes, whose expertise brightens my daily life; Julien from Formia and his exceptional products; flavor masters Matt from Firefly BBQ, the Spice Brigade, Angus & Oink, and the Martin sauces. And of course, the indispensable Vincent Jonard from Grill O'Bois.

My deepest thanks go to Thomas, Jérôme, and Philippe, whose passion for cooking has been shared with me along the way. Their presence and support in our projects have enriched my life in ways I could never fully describe.

This adventure has grown beyond just a business; it has become a story woven with deep human connections and extraordinary relationships. Remarkable men and women—partners, collaborators, friends—have shaped my journey, and their support has added immeasurable value to my life.

To Mahesh, my soul brother, partner in countless achievements, and for the victories still to come. To Niran, who proudly carries the torch and keeps our legacy alive. To Geeth, the passionate one, whose contagious smile lights up every room. And to Joe and Deepan, who have been with me through every step of this adventure—I am infinitely grateful. Their dedication, friendship, and support have been the foundation of this journey, and I extend all my gratitude and affection to them.

The Art of Barbecue: Techniques & Recipes,
from Appetizers to Desserts
Thierry Cornuet

Illustrations
Océane Meklemberg

Graphic Design & Layout
Pierre Manas

U.S. Edition Publisher & Creative Director
Ilona Oppenheim

U.S. Edition Publishing Director
Jessica Faroy

U.S. Edition Art Director & Cover Designer
Jefferson Quintana

U.S. Edition Editorial Director
Lisa McGuinness

U.S. Edition Typesetter
Morgane Leoni

Printed and bound in China by
Artron Art (Group) Co., Ltd.

The Art of Barbecue was first published in the United States
by Tra Publishing, 2025. Text and recipes copyright © 2025
by Thierry Cornuet. *L'art du Barbecue* first published
in 2024 by Hachette Livre (Marabout).

ISBN: 978-1-962098-21-2

This product is made of FSC®-certified
and other controlled material.
Tra Publishing is committed to sustainability
in its materials and practices.

MIX
Paper | Supporting
responsible forestry
FSC® C019910

Tra Publishing
245 NE 37th Street
Miami, FL 33137
trapublishing.com

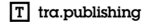

1 2 3 4 5 6 7 8 9 10